ROCKSCHOOL 2

ELECTRONICS, KEYBOARDS AND VOCALS

ROCKSCHOOL 2

ELECTRONICS, KEYBOARDS AND VOCALS

Edited by **Chris Lent**

A Fireside Book

Published by Simon & Schuster, Inc.

New York   London   Toronto   Sydney   Tokyo

Copyright © 1987 by Educational Broadcasting Corporation
All rights reserved
including the right of reproduction
in whole or in part in any form.
A FIRESIDE BOOK
Published by Simon & Schuster, Inc.
Simon & Schuster Building
Rockefeller Center
1230 Avenue of the Americas
New York, NY 10020
FIRESIDE and colophon are registered trademarks of Simon & Schuster, Inc.
Designed by BLACKBIRCH GRAPHICS, INC.
Manufactured in the United States of America

10 9 8 7 6 5 4 3 2 1

Library of Congress Cataloging-in-Publication Data
Rockschool 2.

"A Fireside book."
1. Rock music — Instruction and study.   2. Musical
instruments, Electronic — Instruction and study.
3. Keyboard instruments — Instruction and study.
I. Lent, Chris.
MT170.R63 1987   784.5'4'007   87-14941
ISBN 0-671-64580-3

CONTENTS

Introduction

Welcome to the second *ROCK-SCHOOL* book. For those of you who don't already know and for those of you who might need reminding, *ROCKSCHOOL* is a BBC TV show that explores the techniques, technology and musical vocabulary needed to play in a band.

ROCKSCHOOL began by looking at guitar, bass and drums, and how they worked together to produce the sounds and styles of rock — from blues and rock'n'roll to funk, heavy metal and reggae. Now, presenters Deirdre Cartwright (guitar), Geoff Nicholls (drums), Henry Thomas (bass) and new recruit Alastair Gavin (keyboards), have joined forces with writer and musician Julian Colbeck to investigate the ways in which keyboards, synthesizers and 'new' technology have changed the face of modern music. Also covered are lead and harmony vocals — a vital aspect of

any band's sound. The voice, after all, is an instrument too, and to get it sounding good you have to work at it.

As with the first book, comments are included from some of the leading players featured in the *ROCKSCHOOL* TV series:

TONY BANKS (*Genesis*); GRAHAM BONNET (*Alcatrazz*); BILL BRUFORD (*ex-Yes, King Crimson*); VINCE CLARKE (*Erasure*); OMAR HAKIM (*Weather Report*); JAN HAMMER; HERBIE HANCOCK; MICHAEL McDONALD; JIMMY SOMERVILLE and RICHARD COLES (*The Communards*); ANDY SUMMERS (*The Police*); MIDGE URE (*Ultravox*) . . . and guest vocalist JULIET ROBERTS from one of Britain's hottest jazz-soul acts, *Working Week*.

The book is designed to be used partly as a reference, partly as a

practical guide, and partly as a music tutor. Although divided into four main sections on hardware, playing and programming, vocals, arrangement and song structure, the book is in *modular* form. You don't *have* to start on page one if you don't want to. With the table of contents as your guide, you can dip in anywhere to check a fact or pick up something new. You can ignore the text and simply follow the music examples. You can even just look at the pictures!

Because learning to play rock is still largely a trial and error process, different people have different needs and different gaps in their understanding. Use this book to make up your *own* rock tuition course. We can't tell you how to do it. Only you can do that for yourself. Happy Hunting.

CHRIS LENT

1 Music Basics

Below is an outline of the music notation systems used in this book — bass and treble clef; standard drum notation; guitar tablature; and box diagrams — and a basic explanation of some of the terms referred to in the text. It is by no means intended to be a comprehensive guide to the rudiments of music.

Rock tends to be played by ear, with musicians relying on improvisation and inspiration to get them through. However, even the most basic knowledge of musical rudiments will help you in riffing, soloing, and rhythm work, and it is essential to songwriting and arrangement. Music theory can't be avoided and shouldn't be feared.

NOTES, SCALES AND CHORDS

All Western music is based on 12 notes, each a fixed interval apart in pitch. These 12 notes have names. Seven of them are named after the first seven letters of the alphabet — A, B, C, D, E, F, G. The other five notes fall between these in pitch and are said to be either sharp or flat, depending on whether you are ascending to or descending from one of the 'alphabet notes.' The keyboard gives a strong visual image of the system since the white keys are the alphabet notes and the black ones are the sharps or flats. (See p. 10)

These notes are further subdivided into patterns of *tones* and *semi-tones* called *scales*. There are different types of scales, but those most commonly used are made up of eight notes. The eighth is the same as the first note of the scale, but higher in pitch, and is called the *octave*. The two most basic scales are the major and minor. They sound different because each has a distinct set of intervals between the notes. Starting on C, for example, the major scale step pattern looks like this: *(See Fig. 1)*

The C minor scale step pattern, meanwhile, looks like this: *(Fig. 2)*

You can start a major or minor scale on any note so long as you conform to the appropriate step-pattern.

Each note of the scale is numbered — first, second, third etc., and by combining different scale notes and playing them simultaneously, you get *chords*. Simple chords are called *triads*. They're made up of three notes — the first (or root), the third, and the fifth. You can invert chords by playing these three in a different order (the third-fifth-first combination, for example, is called the *first inversion*). You can also extend chords by adding other notes from the scale — such as the sixth or seventh — and leaving notes from the triad out.

(If you are not already conversant with the major, minor, and blues scales, and with the structure of basic chords, you should refer to our companion volume *ROCKSCHOOL I — Guitar, Bass, Drums*).

THE STAFF

Music is usually written on or in between five horizontal lines known as the *staff*. The notes on the staff indicate both the *pitch* and the *rhythm* of the music. *(See Fig. 3)*

Pitch

The pitch of a note on the staff is shown by its position relative to a *clef* sign placed at the beginning of each line of music. There are two clefs:

Fig. 4

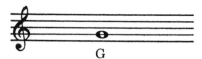

G

The treble (or G) clef is used for guitar and the notes usually played by a keyboard player's right hand.

Fig. 5

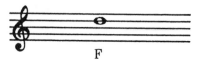

F

The bass (or F) clef is used for bass, the keyboard player's left hand, and sometimes for drums.

Fig. 1

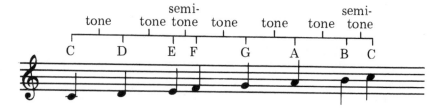

Fig. 2

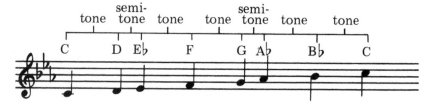

Fig. 3

These clefs each define pitch as follows:

Fig. 6

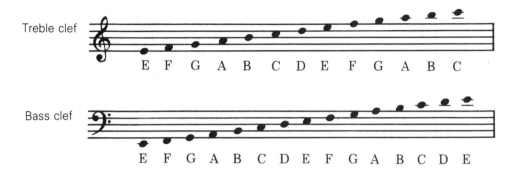

Treble clef

E F G A B C D E F G A B C

Bass clef

E F G A B C D E F G A B C D E

As you can see, notes that go beyond the scope of the five-line staff are written on their own *leger lines*.

Pitch can also be indicated by the use of 'sharp' or 'flat' symbols. A sharp sign # *raises* the pitch of a note by a semi-tone or half step. *(See Fig. 7)*

This is the equivalent of one fret on the guitar and bass, and one key (usually from white to black or vice versa, but see diagram below) on a keyboard instrument. A flat sign ♭ *lowers* the pitch of a note by a half step. You will often see sharps or flats grouped together on the staff at the beginning of a piece of music, just after the clef. This grouping is called the *key signature*. It establishes the key you are playing in and indicates that the notes referred to are always played in that key.

Fig. 7

F♯ G♭ G♯ A♭ A♯ B♭ C♯ D♭ D♯ E♭

The F♯ marked here shows that the key is G major.

Fig. 8

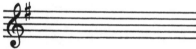

The B♭ shown here reveals that the key is G minor.

Fig. 9

The sharps or flats in a key signature always occur in the same order, as shown below: *(See Fig. 10)*

If a note is unsharpened or un-flattened, a 'natural' sign is written in front of it. This takes effect for one bar only. It looks like this:

Fig. 11

Fig. 10

Number of sharps	Note(s) affected	Treble clef example	Bass clef example
1	F		
2	F C		
3	F C G		
4	F C G D		
5	F C G D A		
6	F C G D A E		
7	F C G D A E B		

Number of flats	Note(s) affected	Treble clef example	Bass clef example
1	B		
2	B E		
3	B E A		
4	B E A D		
5	B E A D G		
6	B E A D G C		
7	B E A D G C F		

Below are shown the key and fret pitches of a keyboard, guitar and bass, all in standard tuning:

Fig. 12

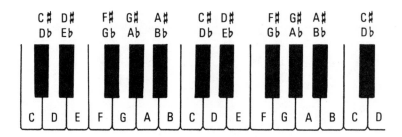
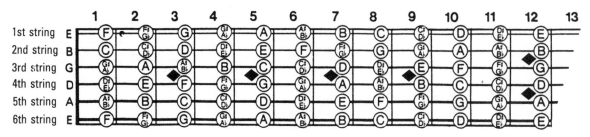

Fig. 13

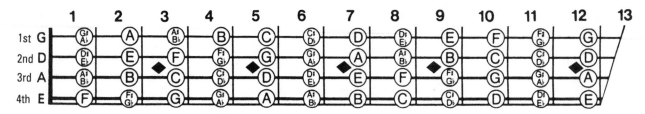

Fig. 14

Rhythm

Staffs are divided into equal sections, called bars or *measures*, each signifying a period of time. Each measure contains a number of beats or pulses, fixed by the *time signature* at the beginning of the music. This consists of an upper and lower number, which between them show the number of beats within each bar, and the time value allotted to each beat.

In common with most of rock, the musical illustrations in this book are in 4/4 time. This means that each bar contains four beats each of which lasts the length of a *quarter note* (see below).

Note Values

Note values represent the length of time that each individual note is sounded. Because rock music is so dance-oriented, the notes favored tend to be reasonably short. This gives the music an up-tempo, driving feel. Even so, it's unusual to get more than sixteen notes to the bar. And you often encounter long passages involving one note held over a bar or even longer. The note values which therefore appear most frequently in rock 4/4 time are as follows:

(Count 1 2 3 4)
* The *whole note* (semibreve), which lasts for four beats or quarter notes:

* The *half note* (minim), which lasts for two beats or quarter notes:

* The *quarter note* (crotchet), which indicates one beat; there are usually four to the bar:

* The *eighth note* (quaver), which indicates a half-beat:

* The *sixteenth note* (semi-quaver); there are four of these to each beat:

Fig. 15

To get a feeling for the ways in which different note values 'speed up' or 'slow down' the music, it's worth practicing the line below:

Note values can be modified, and this is indicated by a variety of additional symbols. A dot placed after the note, for example, will increase its length by half:

Two notes linked together by a curved line or *tie* show that the value of the first note is increased by the value of the second:

Just as important as note values are those signs indicating an equivalent period of silence, where you don't play. These are called *rests*. When playing in a band, remember that what you *don't* play contributes as much to the music as what you *do* play. So pay particular attention to rest signs. They look like this:

whole note (one measure) rest

half note rest

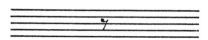

quarter note rest

eighth note rest

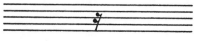

sixteenth note rest

Other time signatures are associated with other styles, but can also occur in rock. The 'swing' of some jazz, blues, and country and western music, for example, is provided by a 12/8 time signature. This consists of 12 eighth notes to the bar, split into groups of three per beat: *1*-2-3, *2*-2-3, *3*-2-3, *4*-2-3, and so on.

Triplets
Triplets form the basis of many rock beats (boogie, for example), and are often used in rhythmic *syncopations*. They consist of notes grouped into patterns of three played 'across' the beat, and look like this:

This *eighth note triplet* consists of three evenly spaced notes played in the time of a quarter note beat.

This *quarter note triplet* is made up of three evenly spaced notes played in the time of a half note beat.

TABLATURE
This system is useful for guitarists and bassists because it not only shows you *what* to play, but *how* to play it. Each line in the diagram below represents a string — six for guitar and four for bass — with the first string on the top line. The numbers show you which fret to finger, and the other symbols indicate different playing techniques. So this example tells you to fret the C on the third (G) string, and hammer on to a D:

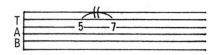

Common technique symbols are:

bend

pull-off

hammer-on

vibrato

slide

harmonic

T

tap

T

thumb
(usually for bass only)

✖

choke
(usually for bass only)

BOX DIAGRAMS

This is another method for indicating fingering. It's especially useful for describing chord shapes. As with tablature, the horizontal lines represent the strings. But this time, the frets are drawn in and numbered at the top. The numbers on the strings tell you which fingers to use. *O* means play this string open; *X* means don't play this string.

Fig. 16

A D major chord is illustrated.

DRUM NOTATION

In this book, the five-line staff and standard note values are used. Position on the staff indicates different drums, as follows: *(See Fig. 17)*

Cymbals, hi-hats, cabassas and cowbells etc., are notated on top or above the staff, as follows: *(See Fig. 18)*

Fig. 17

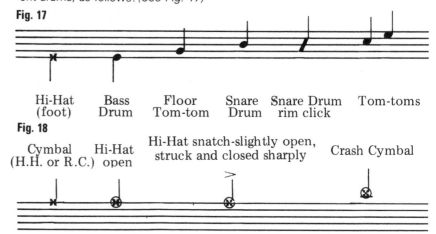

Hi-Hat (foot) Bass Drum Floor Tom-tom Snare Drum Snare Drum rim click Tom-toms

Fig. 18

Cymbal (H.H. or R.C.) Hi-Hat open Hi-Hat snatch-slightly open, struck and closed sharply Crash Cymbal

SOUND BASICS

Every day we hear a great variety of sounds — voices, planes flying overhead, a tap dripping, and records playing. Even when they occur simultaneously, there seems to be no limit to the ear's ability to distinguish one sound from another.

But what's all this got to do with rock'n'roll? Time was, when you joined a band, you turned up, plugged in, and tuned out. But with the advent of synthesizers, samplers and digital gadgetry, musicians now have unprecedented opportunities to create and manipulate sounds and effects. So it's important to understand something of what sound *is* if you want to develop your programming skills.

Sound Waves

Sound is the *movement of the air* caused by an object vibrating. This movement takes the form of 'waves,' similar to the effect of a stone hitting the surface of a pond and causing circular ripples. When sound waves pass into the human ear they cause the ear drum to vibrate sympathetically. The nervous system interprets these vibrations and helps the brain to identify them.

The brain's job is made easier by the fact that sound waves come in many different shapes and sizes. Rounded waves give softer tone colors, while jagged waves give harder, brighter tones. And wave *form* is dependent on three basic characteristics: *pitch, timbre* or sound quality, loudness or *amplitude*. By changing these characteristics you change the nature of the sound you make. Pitch, for example, is signified by wave *length* — the distance between two peaks in the sound wave. The shorter the wave length, the higher the pitch of the note. *(See Fig. 19)*

When different pitches are compared, the higher sounds are seen to produce a greater number of waves per second than the lower sounds. The number of waves corresponds exactly to the number of vibrations causing the sound, and their frequency is measured in *Hertz (Hz)*. For example, 100 HZ = 100 vibrations per second. Doubling the frequency will raise the pitch of a sound by an octave.

The quality or *timbre* of a note is represented by the *shape* of the sound wave. The simplest shape and purest tone is represented by the sine wave. If you combine several of these at different frequencies, you get *harmonics*. These produce more interesting distortions: the triangular wave, which gives a flute-like sound; the sawtooth, which is a little like brass; the square wave, which gives a thinner, reedier sound; and so on. *(See Fig. 20)*

The loudness of a note, meanwhile, is shown by the height or *amplitude* of the sound wave. The higher the wave, the louder the sound. *(See Fig. 21)*

But loudness is not just a question of volume. Every note you play goes through a cycle of amplitude, consisting of the following parameters: *Attack* (how quickly the note sounds), *Decay* (how quickly it dies away after reaching peak volume), *Sustain* (volume level of note while played), *Release* (how quickly the note dies away after the note has been played). And it is the combination of these elements from the beginning of the sound until the point where it fades completely that helps to give each sound its unique character.

For example, if you play a violin with a bow, the volume gradually increases and the tone color and pitch also change slightly. This is what makes a violin sound like a violin. On the other hand, if you were able to sustain a piano note indefinitely instead of allowing it to decay naturally, you would have difficulty in distinguishing its sound from that of a flute.

Collectively these changes in pitch, volume and tone color over a given period of time are called *envelopes*. You can compare different envelopes graphically: *(See Fig. 22)*

Both analog and digital synthesizers (see p. 98) take an electric current, turn it into a sound, and allow you to shape it by altering the waveforms and envelopes of the sounds produced. (For more on synths and how to program them, see p.101).

Fig. 19

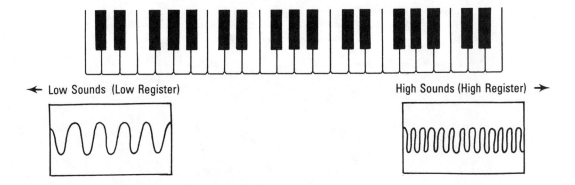

← Low Sounds (Low Register)   High Sounds (High Register) →

Fig. 20

WAVE FORM	NAME	TONE COLOR	INSTRUMENT IT IS SIMILAR TO
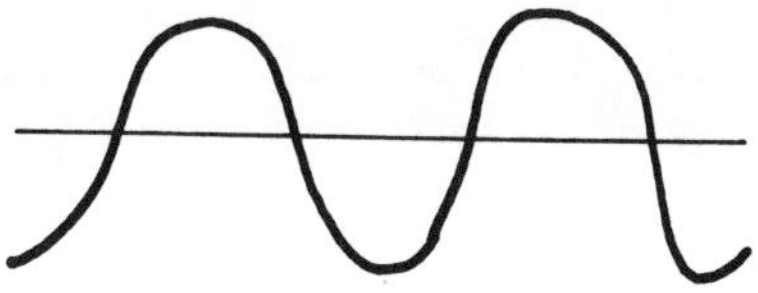	SINE WAVE	SOFT	FLUTE, WHISTLE
	SAW-TOOTH WAVE	BRIGHT	VIOLIN, TRUMPET
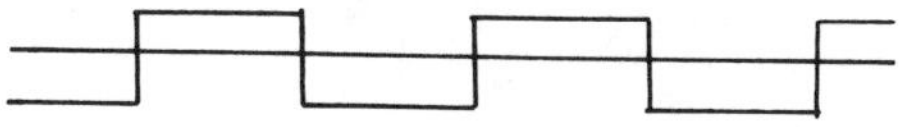	SQUARE WAVE	THIN	CLARINET, OBOE

Fig. 21

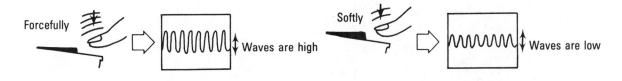

Forcefully ⇨ Waves are high   Softly ⇨ Waves are low

Fig. 22

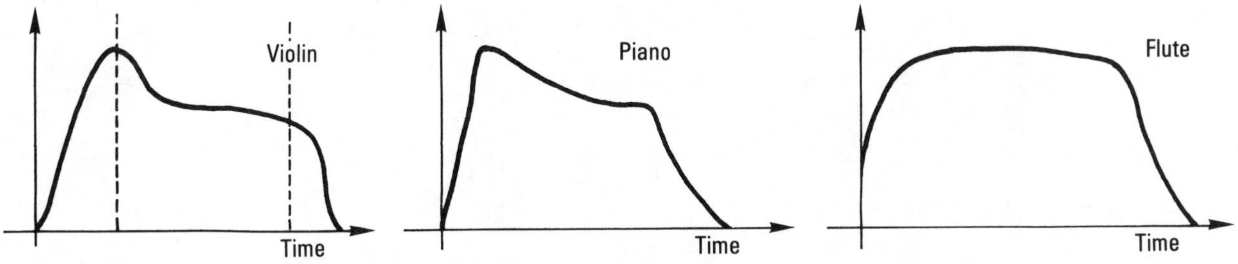

Violin   Piano   Flute

Time   Time   Time

2 Hardware History

Billy Joel playing a CP70

KEYBOARDS

Introduction

Originally, keyboard instruments didn't even *have* keyboards. In medieval times, for example, church organs consisted of pipes that were opened and closed by large, heavy levers that had to be punched with a clenched (and gloved) fist. This was hardly conducive to refined performance and sometime during the Middle Ages this method was replaced by a system of keys. The first keyboard simply offered a continuous run of notes that divided an octave into seven, i.e., white notes only. Since these early keyboards had no sharps or flats, names were usually etched onto the keys so you could identify the notes. The first seven letters of the alphabet was the obvious choice.

In time these seven divisions were judged insufficient (the interval between F and B being the first to be thought discordant—play in fourths starting from C, using white notes only, and you'll see why!). Having slotted in B flat, other 'black' keys soon followed; and by the mid-14th century the fully chromatic keyboard as we know it today had arrived.

The keyboard is simply a device for giving your hands control over four basic methods of making pitched sounds. Three of these have been around since the dawn of time: striking, plucking, blowing. The fourth is more recent: electronic signal generation.

Based on a genuine synthesis of technologies developed for percussion, wind, and plucked-string instruments, the earliest pianos were lucky not to have been called synthesizers!

It didn't take too long for makers of plucked string instruments like zithers, psalteries, and monochords (a stand alone, single-stringed instrument with a movable bridge, rather like a pedal steel guitar), to catch on to this new form of control and soon a new breed of instrument that used levered keys to pluck strings appeared, the first being the clavichord (*clavis* meaning key, *chorde* meaning string).

The final breakthrough came in the 18th century, when it was proved that striking the strings with felt hammers was far more controllable and expressive a system than plucking. And so the piano, finally classified as a percussion instrument, was born.

The Piano
In 1698 Bartolomeo Cristofori, keeper of instruments at the Florentine Court of the Medici, started to design a harpsichord that would play both loud and soft, applying the principles of the dulcimer (a four-sided box of strings using hammers held in the hand to generate sound). By 1700 the prototype had been built, being followed by a perfected model in 1709. Cristofori's invention was created as a result of a specific request from Prince Ferdinand, who wished to make the harpsichord more expressive. What resulted was the creation of a totally new instrument allowing dynamics and timbre to be controlled by the per-

former through the keyboard. The first 'piano action' had been invented. The basic design and action of Cristofori's piano was so complete that it has survived for hundreds of years.

The first upright pianos ('parlor' pianos) were introduced from Germany around 1770, made by Christian Ernst Friederici at Gera.

Between 1795 and 1830 an instrument called the orphica was produced (looking remarkably like a portable synthesizer controller such as the Moog Liberation or Clavitar), which could be slung across the shoulder and played almost anywhere, being a miniature acoustic piano with a Viennese-type action. The English called the orphica the

Billy Joel bashes the hell out of a grand piano!

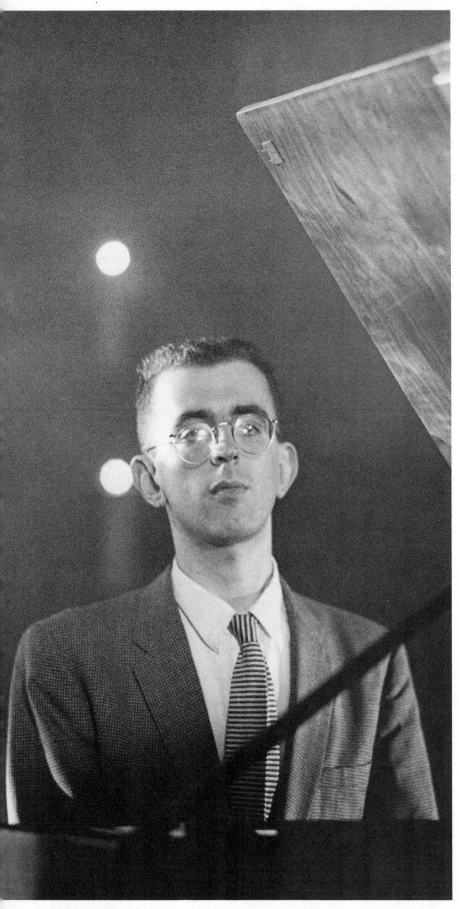

Richard Coles

'weekend piano,' as it could be played outside.

Around 1800, with the growing popularity of piano music, larger and louder pianos were required to cope with bigger venues and audiences. Piano strings became tighter and thicker, making it necessary for structural reinforcement to cope with the additional stress. The first complete iron frames were made by Babcock in 1825 and were soon introduced into other parts of the world, becoming the norm by about 1860.

The modern acoustic piano bears most of the design features of these early instruments, although almost three centuries of improvements have refined it vastly. Despite the technological revolution in keyboard instrument design that has taken place this century, the piano remains the first love of many musicians.

Touch sensitivity is an important part of getting expression out of an instrument. The way you pluck the strings of a guitar or bass will change the quality of the sound from loud to soft, or from bright to percussive. With its weighted, wooden keys, the acoustic piano requires more physical effort to play than the plastic keys of later electronic instruments, but it also gives you greater control over the nuances of the sound. With quieter pieces, for example, you can employ different stroke techniques, with your hands either 'pushing' into the keys as you play to produce a slightly non-focused, almost string-type sound; or with your hands 'pulling' away from the keys to produce a clear, more bell-like sound. If you let your hands fall onto the keys, pushing from the shoulder, you can get almost

"I like playing the piano so much because it's such a versatile instrument. You have an immediate physical control over the mechanics of it which means that if you want to go loud you can go loud and it's not a question of bumping up a level — it's purely a mechanical response. So you do get an immediate live feeling from a piano which you don't really get off an electronic instrument. Even though there are lots of touch sensitive keyboards and all that, they never have the direct feel that a piano has."
RICHARD COLES, The Communards.

"Basically, a piano key is on the path to the actual thing that produces the sound, which is the string. The way you hit the key, the force and the speed, determines how the sound is going to be. Synthesizer keys are completely different. They're just switches. And at this point, you still can't quite get all the nuances out of a synthesizer with your fingers as you can out of an acoustic piano. But that day will come!"

HERBIE HANCOCK

Jan Hammer

"Playing early synthesizer keyboards was quite different to what I'd been used to on piano. On the other hand it made me do different things. It's quite nice to be shocked — it makes you a more interesting player. For instance, changing from the discipline of the piano — sitting there practicing scales and études — to the silly, weightless keyboard of the MiniMoog, made me think in a totally unorthodox way."

JAN HAMMER

brass-like stabs. And a very subtle technique known as *after touch* can be used to dampen the note or to give the faintest repeat (see p.123 for synthesizer after touch technique). Although these techniques tend to apply more to classical playing than to rock, they do give some idea of the unique versatility of the acoustic piano.

The next major breakthrough in keyboard technology came with the harnessing of electricity. During the early years of this century, in the wake of the gramaphone and telephone, came electric and electronic pianos and organs.

The electrification of pianos dates back to the 1930s, when instruments such as the Crea-Tone flirted briefly with success. But it wasn't until the '60s that three instruments appeared that would change piano playing forever. As testament to their importance, their individual sounds have remained copied long after the instruments themselves have ceased to be made or used. They are the **Fender Rhodes**, the **Wurlitzer EP200**, and the **Hohner Clavinet.**

Harold Rhodes was a flying instructor with the US Air force during World War II. He built his first

Chick Corea playing a Fender Rhodes

ELECTRIC/ELECTRONIC PIANOS

An electric piano is an *electrified* piano, in other words sounds are produced by some form of conventional hammer action, and then amplified. An electronic piano is one that produces piano-type tones purely through *electronics*. And it used to be as simple as that: electric pianos were worth buying since they retained one of the piano's prime features — touch sensitivity — and electronic pianos, blessed with floppy actions and nasty, buzzing, 'electronic' tones, were generally to be given a wide berth. Today, thanks to advanced digital technology almost the reverse is true.

electric piano to be used in a neighboring hospital's rehabilitation program, out of old B17 aircraft spare parts. Always more inventor than businessman, Rhodes took some twenty years to get his brainchild onto the market in 1965, thanks to pioneer guitar and amp designer Leo Fender.

From 1965 until its deletion in 1984, Rhodes' basic concept of using rubber hammers to hit tines (thin, spun-metal rods) instead of strings remained unchanged. Although a number of models were produced (such as the Stage 73, and the Suitcase 88 — with a built-under amplification system) all had

that same magically smooth, 'jazzy' sound that has become synonymous with the term "electric piano." Herbie Hancock almost built his reputation around the instrument. Today the Rhodes legacy remains as one of the most sought-after piano-type sounds for synths, samplers, and all current digital pianos.

Wurlitzer, of course, is a name synonymous with organs. But in the 1950s one of their engineers, B.F. Meissner, hit upon the idea of making a piano by adapting an organ-type system of reeds. Meissner's reeds were metal, and though varying in length for the dif-

ferent pitches, were fine tuned using the tortuous method of dabbing blobs of solder onto the ends of the reeds. Needless to say, tuning a Wurlitzer piano has never been easy. The piano was launched in 1955 and enjoyed considerable success for 20 years or more, due not only to its distinctive sound (Supertramp's "Dreamer"), but also to its size, portability, and the fact that it housed a small stereo speaker system — as well as a headphone socket. If you had to sum up the Rhodes versus the 'Wurli,' then the Rhodes was best suited to smooth jazz and the Wurli to rock.

Wurlitzer piano

Clavinet

The third seminal instrument to emerge from the '50s and '60s was the Hohner Clavinet. Designed by Ernst Zacharias, the Clavinet's most lasting manisfestation was the D6, launched in 1971 and used to devastating effect on Stevie Wonder's all-time classic, "Superstition."

The Clavinet employs a fairly conventional hammer-to-string system, the sound passed on to the amplifier via an almost limitless number of pickup configurations, selected by rocker switches on the control panel. The sad fact is that a 'Clavinet' sound is food and drink to the average synthesizer. It has been copied and adapted mercilessly, to the point where anyone wanting to *own* a real Clavinet would now be classed as a nut. Equally sad, however, is the fact that a real Clavinet is a far more versatile instrument than was ever credited. It was touch sensitive, you could bend notes with added

"The acoustic piano is not a blending instrument. This is why it's not used as an integral part of a symphony orchestra — at least that's what I was told when I was a kid. It's really a solo instrument. But a Rhodes sound is characteristic of something like a guitar and something like a vibraphone — mellow but with an edge to it. It blends much more easily into what the rhythm section is doing. The other thing of course is that you can turn it up. When I first played a Rhodes, I had only previously played acoustic piano. So the fact I could turn up the sound and the drummer could play just as loud behind me as he did behind the trumpet player was wonderful."

HERBIE HANCOCK

pressure, and a range of tones from rich and resonant to thin and clipped were possible using different pickup arrangements and levels of string-damping.

Throughout the '70s these three instruments, aided and abetted by the **Hohner Pianet** (which employed a very odd system of plucked metal reeds using suction pads), dominated the scene for the professional and semi-professional keyboard player.

Meanwhile, notably from Italy, there came a vast number of electronic pianos made by such companies as Crumar and Bontempi. Few, if any, made any real impression outside the lucrative in-home market.

Even though the Rhodes, Wurlitzer, and Clavinet were great instruments in their time, none even tried to emulate the sound of a real acoustic piano. Those wanting a real acoustic piano sound on stage had to resort to miking one up — invariably a less than satisfactory solution.

So when Yamaha launched the CP70 and CP80 in 1978, both were an instant success. The CP pianos are simply regular pianos with strings and hammer action that are blessed with purpose-designed pickups. They fold into reasonably portable, although rather heavy, units and can be connected to any amplifier like any ordinary electronic keyboard. However they still require tuning — like any ordinary piano! — and are not cheap.

The situation changed in 1983 when Yamaha, not content with turning the synth market upside down with the DX7, precipitated the current digital piano revolution with the PF10 and PF15. Although neither were exactly brilliant at re-

producing the sound of an acoustic piano, the range of electric piano tones (thanks to FM, as on the DX synths — see p. 40) was brilliant enough to show the Rhodes a clean pair of heels. More versatile, lighter (just!), blessed with an internal amplification system, and without any tuning problems, the PF pianos became standard equipment almost overnight.

As with synths, it took manufacturers some time to catch up with Yamaha. But by 1986, with various designs available from the likes of Roland and Korg, the digital piano had truly come of age.

Digital Pianos

There are two basic types of digital piano: those whose sounds are created *digitally* out of thin air, so to speak; and those whose sounds are based on samples of a real piano. Both normally sport weighted keys to re-create the action of a real piano.

Leading examples in the 'out of thin air' category include the Roland RD-1000, and the Yamaha PF 70/80. In the sampled category one would have to include all the Technics PX Series, the Ensoniq SDP-1, and the Korg SG-1.

Of course the current fascination with samplers theoretically means that all you have to do is sample your favorite Bosendorfer and blip!, there you've got it. Well, not quite. For a start sampling is never quite as simple as it seems (see p. 76), and secondly a truly mammoth amount of memory would be needed to take into account all the nuances of a genuine piano sound as it slowly changes, through time, after you play a note.

ELECTRONIC ORGANS

For hundreds of years organs were used almost exclusively in churches, but in the late 19th and early 20th centuries they began to appear in music halls, cinemas, places of entertainment. The reason for both is that the organ is an incredibly versatile beast, at the same time capable of thunderous noises to put the fear of God into you, and of soothing, gentle, magical sounds to calm your fractured nerves. Until the synthesizer arrived, the organ was by far the most versatile of keyboard instruments.

Roland RD-1000

Shortly before World War II, Laurens Hammond adapted the Telharmonium's rotating disk system of producing sound into what is known as the tone wheel. In simple terms, the tone wheel injects a constantly-shifting human feel into the sounds by playing around with a vast number of harmonics. Although organs are not touch sensitive instruments, the Hammond sound is incredibly expressive, and it was the natural choice for jazz musicians in the '50s and '60s, from Jimmy Smith, to Booker T. Jones, to Georgie Fame.

Part of its appeal also lies in its amplification system, the Leslie cabinet. The Leslie speaker's appeal lies in its unique Doppler effect (the effect of pitch changing on a moving sound — a police car's siren as it flies by), created by two speakers rotating at different speeds.

Hammonds and Leslies were *de rigeur* for all rock keyboard players in the '60s and '70s. Keith Emerson, Jon Lord of Deep Purple, Steve Winwood — practically built their careers on them.

If the Hammond was king for jazz and rock musicians, the Vox Continental, with its thinner, cutting sound, was the instrument for pop bands like the Dave Clark Five in the '60s, and once again for bands like Madness a decade later.

Although the organ *sound* continues to be used today, organs themselves have not fared so well. The problem is two-fold. First, most organs (and especially the Hammonds) are bulky and heavy. Second, the organ sound is reasonably simple for a synthesizer to re-create. The result: very few dedicated 'rock' organs continue to be made; and almost every synthesizer continues to bristle with an array of organ presets. Nevertheless, there remains something indefinably special about the Hammond/Leslie combination, to which the sound of rock owes a great debt.

More importantly comes the question of feel. No matter how crafty, careful, or expert manufacturers have become, none have recreated the perfect facsimile of an acoustic piano keyboard. And this is fundamentally important, since much of what you play on a piano depends upon how the piano feels. At one extreme, an electric piano that has an organ-type keyboard and doesn't respond to touch sensitivity is nigh on impossible to play *like a piano*. Sure you can play it. But you'll end up playing synthesizer parts, not piano parts. And sadly, even on the best modern examples, like the Technics PX1 and Roland RD-1000, pianists will find themselves adapting their performances to suit.

And in fact the best known 'rock' organ, the Hammond, owes its existence to one of the first attempts at making a synthesizer, the Telharmonium.

THE CLASSIC ROCK ORGAN SOUND

*key click (dirt in the contacts!)
*harmonics
*movement (continuous shifting of harmonics, pitch, etc.)

Stevie Wonder ▷

Booker T. Jones

SYNTHESIZERS

Early Synths

While the organ ruled supreme as *the* electronic instrument both on stage and in the home, a few designers were tinkering with more outlandish forms of pitched sound generation — synthesizers.

The first instrument to call itself a synthesizer was made by RCA in 1954 and was designed by two Americans, Harry F. Olson and Herbert Belar. The enormous and unwieldy RCA Mk 1 never really saw the light of day and was quickly replaced by the RCA Mk 2 (only slightly less cumbersome), which was duly installed in New York's Columbia-Princeton studio at a cost of $100,000.

However, electronic instruments of one sort or another had been around since the turn of the century, and *mechanical* instruments (of which most of the early electronic instruments were simply electrified versions) date back almost as far the organ and piano themselves. It seems that no sooner had 'an instrument' been invented than someone else invented a model that played itself.

By the turn of the century, scientists the world over were busy putting their new-found awareness of the potential of electricity into practical, musical use. In 1903, Sir Charles Parsons demonstrated his Auxetophone — a sort of giant PA

system. In 1906, the Canadian inventor Thaddeus Cahill actually built the Telharmonium, the 200-ton monster he'd patented ten years previously, and in the '20s and '30s a whole stream of French, German, and Russian research scientists labored over such bizarre contraptions as the Etherophone, Sperophone, Partituro-phone, and Trautonium.

Early instruments like the 'Automatically Operating Musical Instrument of the Electronic Oscillation Type' designed in 1929 by two French inventors, Edouard Couplex and Joseph Givelet, often used hole-punched tape reader systems — a concept designed by an-

Keith Emerson

"I think of synthesizers as tools for making instruments. A piano is only one instrument. A synth is whatever you've programmed into it for that moment. And its use musically is determined by your concept of that sound in relation to what other music is going on around it. So where it goes is determined by the person playing it."

HERBIE HANCOCK

other Frenchman, Jacquard, as far back as 1790, for use with weaving machines. This was subsequently applied to musical instruments in the 19th century through the player piano and mechanical harmonium.

If such instruments have a familiar ring to them, so they should. They all used the binary system (in other words the tape reader responds to one of *two* things on the tape: seeing a hole or not seeing a hole) and were, in effect, computers. Couplex and Givelet used this system to store data concerning pitch, volume, tone, etc. that was applied to a number of oscillators and filters to produce music, electronic music.

'Electronic music' became so defined in Germany in the '50s to set itself apart from *musique concrete* — a related but significantly different form of musical manipulation that was becoming all the rage

in France (*musique concrete* being based on recordings of natural, real, or 'concrete' sounds stored, initially, on disc; in effect, early sampling) — both of which were pioneered by radio stations, NWDR in Cologne and ORTF in Paris.

But not all 'pre-synthesizers' were like Couplex and Givelet's creation. Others used a far cruder form of control over oscillators, such as waving your arms about over a row of antennae (to change pitch) as seen on an outlandish instrument called the Etherophone, built by a Russian named Lev Termin in 1920; and the Ondes Musicale from Maurice Martinot, built in 1928.

Trautonium

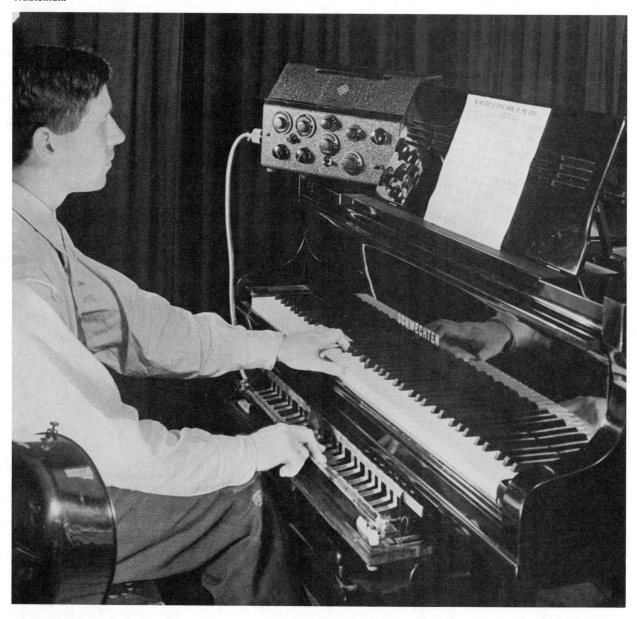

Keith Emerson

The Ondes Musicale went on to become the Ondes Martinot, and though a name still bandied about in highbrow electronic music circles, it fell into obscurity pretty quickly. The Etherophone, however, went on to become the Theramin, which was used by such leading musical minds of the '20s and '30s as Schillinger and Pashchenko. But it wasn't all highbrow stuff. Remember that whinnying, spacy sound on The Beach Boys' hit "Good Vibrations"? Well, that was a Theramin too. In fact Theramins became something of a cult, and in the late '50s and early '60s you could even buy them in kit form— from a young Cornell physics student named Robert Moog.

Moog, or rather Dr. Moog as he became having gained his Ph.D, teamed up with an electronic music composer named Herb Deutsch in 1963 and they established a company producing voltage-controlled synthesizer modules based on the three essential ingredients of sounds: pitch, tone, and volume, from which they produced the VCO, the VCF, and the VCA (see p. 98).

What turned this rather esoteric exercise into a major industry was an LP made in 1967 called "Switched On Bach" on which the performer, Walter Carlos, had exclusively used the Moog modules. The album was an astounding success, proving, at last, that synthesizers could produce music in the accepted, mainstream sense of the word. But synthesizer modules at that time were bulky and expensive. Few musicians could afford them and even fewer (ELO, Tangerine Dream) could contemplate taking them on the road.

In 1968, Moog began work on a more compact, self-contained instrument that would effectively house his modules under one roof. It became the *MiniMoog*, and was launched in 1971 to instant and almost universal acclaim. More than any other single new instrument, the MiniMoog helped to define the sounds of the '70s, with players as diverse as Keith Emerson, Chick Corea, and Jan Hammer relying heavily upon its distinctive tones. Synthesizers had finally arrived.

Tangerine Dream

Brian Eno on stage with Roxy Music in 1972 with homemade synths.

Synths in the early '70s were monophonic, unprogrammable and lacking touch sensitive keyboards. Players who wanted instant access to different sounds and feels found themselves moving mountains of equipment around from gig to gig. The multi-keyboard player was born.

The MiniMoog

It's easy to think that the Mini-Moog single-handedly kicked the whole notion of synthesizers — as regular instruments — into life. Though the MiniMoog was undoubtedly the most eye-catching and popular of the early portable synths, it was not the only one. The ARP Odyssey, a slimmed-down version of the large modular ARP 2500, was launched in 1972; for years the British company EMS had been producing a series of rather quaint modules and instruments like the VCS-3 and the Synthi A — the latter a synth-in-a-briefcase (only in England!) — and yet another eponymous company, Oberheim, led by Tom Oberheim, began an illustrious career in 1970 with their Ring Modulator.

MiniMoog

During these early years almost all the instruments were monophonic (only able to play one note at a time), and strictly non-programmable (unable to store program patch settings). You had a vast control over sounds, of course, but only one sound could be 'set up' at any one time. However, almost every self-respecting band boasted either a MiniMoog or an Odyssey — usually perched on a Hammond organ or strapped onto a Fender Rhodes piano — and almost invariably, they sounded terrible.

The problems were threefold. Firstly tuning. On the MiniMoog, especially, the oscillators were notoriously unstable and by the end of the second number they'd have drifted unusably.

Next, there was the problem of real-time patch changing. In other words to change sounds you'd have to twiddle a whole sea of control knobs — without anything

"I always dreamt of an instrument that I could do things with like horn players or violinists, or even singers could do. Like bending and sliding notes. Piano didn't seem to give you any room to stretch in that way. And I kept imagining putting things on the piano, like on a harp where you can move the strings. With the organ you could only bend notes if you turned it on and off — the organ didn't like that! So then I tried all kinds of interim solutions like putting devices on electric piano which would give it a bit more stretch. When I finally got my hands on a MiniMoog — that was the instrument. And I knew from that point on, that was my voice."

JAN HAMMER

to help you like a display screen — and, fairly obviously, this was another hazardous pastime. One inadvertent twiddle and you'd be committed to some dreadful racket for the rest of the song!

ARP Odyssey

Finally there was the problem of simply being heard. Keyboard amplification has always required more thought than it's been given and if one image can describe the late '60s/early '70s keyboard scene it is of a keyboard player surrounded by banks of impossibly complicated-looking gear, all of which someone had evidently forgotten to switch on!

This situation persisted until the mid- to late-'70s when, but for a further breakthrough in synth technology, the synthesizer would probably have slipped into obscurity. The breakthrough, of course, was readily available *polyphony:* the capacity to play more than one note at once.

Once again Moog is generally credited with having produced the first polyphonic synthesizer, the PolyMoog, in 1978. But in fact Oberheim got there years earlier with their Synthesizer Expander Modules. Each SEM was a fully operable monophonic instrument and Oberheim had the brainwave of simply re-packaging them linked together as two-, four-, and eight-voice instruments. Once again tun-

ing was a major problem (in fact two, four, or eight major problems!), but on a day when the majority of the SEMs remained at last close to being in tune the Oberheim sounded fantastic.

A lot of fuss was made when the PolyMoog arrived (Keith Emerson had used a prototype on the "Brain Salad Surgery" LP) but frankly it was a pig of an instrument. In spite of a velocity sensitive keyboard, a number of preset sounds, and one memory (of sorts) it just sounded awful, and, mercifully, sank into relative obscurity within a very short space of time.

The Prophet 5

The prime reason for this was the arrival of the father of modern polyphonic synthesizers, the *Prophet-5*, made by yet another American company, then called Sequential Circuits, now simply Sequential.

What set the Prophet-5 apart from all previous synths was its use of *microprocessors*, computer chips that could manage and mem-

orize programming parameters, so that at last synthesizers could compete with (and, of course, ultimately overtake) organs and pianos in offering the keyboard player a glittering array of instantly re-callable, polyphonic sounds. Prophet-5s (and a twin keyboard version, the Prophet-10) can be heard in a lot of late-'70s and early-'80s pop, including "Ghosts" by Japan, "It's My Party" by Dave Stewart and Barbara Gaskin, and "New Life" by Depeche Mode.

Although Sequential got there first, many other companies were working along similar lines and it wasn't long before Oberheim also produced a microprocessor-controlled, dedicated polyphonic synth, the OB-X; and more ominously, Japanese companies such as the giant Yamaha responded with the CS-60 and CS-80.

Until then Japanese keyboards had been seen as strictly low-cost copies, vastly inferior to American-made originals. Japanese instruments also seemed very shrill and harsh, and the Japanese 'ear' was blamed. But western attitudes began to change with the realization

Analog and *digital* are terms often bandied about in music, and it's important to understand the difference between the two when it comes to synthesis.

1. All early synths were analog, i.e., voltage controlled. They created sound by generating an electrical current using oscillators and then shaping it by filtering out certain frequencies.

2. Fully digital synths use computer technology to create much more complex waveforms and therefore more accurate imitations of other instruments. These waveforms are generated mathematically in *binary* code and aren't subject to the degeneration that a voltage-controlled signal suffers by being pushed through a circuit board.

3. This means you get a clearer, cleaner sound than analog synths are able to produce.

Yellow Magic Orchestra using a Prophet-5

Japan

that Japan would, in time, produce synthesizers that were both more reliable and less expensive. The Yamaha CS-80 was soon followed by the Jupiter-4, an early product of a new company, Roland.

Armed with the option of polyphony you'd think that from 1978 keyboard players would have abandoned all thoughts of monophonic synthesizers without a second thought. Wrong. In 1978 a Prophet-5 would set you back some $5500 and a CS-80 nearly $7000. Translate that into current equivalents and you're talking about $15,000 plus. Few keyboard players could even contemplate buying one of the early polyphonic synths.

And from 1978 to 1980 appeared a steady stream of monophonic synths: from America instruments like the MultiMoog, MicroMoog, ARP Prodigy and Pro DGX; from Japan the Yamaha CS-5 and CS-15, Roland SH-1 and SH-2, and Korg MS-10 and MS-20; and from England, an extraordinary little instrument called the Wasp, made by the Oxfordshire-based company Electronic Dream Plant. The Wasp only had a contact keyboard (the keys were simply painted onto a piece of board resting on touch sensitive pads), but it was nonetheless a fully fledged monophonic synth, with a proper complement of oscillators, filters, and envelope generators, plus it had built-in speakers and was battery operable. It was also extremely cheap! Important though the Wasp was, its life-span was brief due to unreliability, and most players' eventual frustration of having to play a 'pretend' keyboard.

The next big breakthrough came in 1982 when Roland produced the Juno-6, and, too quickly for some, the Juno-60. (They were identical save for the 60's addition of 56 memories.) The reason for the breakthrough was low price and a high degree of stability, the latter thanks to the presence of *digitally*-controlled oscillators. Until this time almost all synths, mono or poly, had still been at the mercy of prone-to-drift *voltage*-controlled oscillators.

The final reason for the success of the Juno-60 is far more basic: it just sounds great. Soon Korg came up with their equivalent, the Polysix, and Sequential with the Prophet-600. Oberheim were not convinced by the mass market ap-

proach and continued producing relatively expensive instruments, like the OB-8, until the company went briefly into liquidation.

FM Synthesis and Phase Distortion

Yamaha, meanwhile, was working on a completely new system of synthesis that had nothing to do with VCOs or DCOs, and in 1982 caused considerable merriment amongst their competition by launching a pair of ridiculously expensive synths called the GS-1 and GS-2. Boy had Yamaha got it wrong!

And the following year Yamaha used the same silly FM (Frequency Modulation) digital system of synthesis again, on a pair of reasonably priced synths this time, called the DX7 and DX9. To date, as you probably know, the DX7 has outsold almost any other synth produced by about 10 to 1.

Although the DX7 — the first readily-available digital synth to hit the streets — came out in 1983, it has taken years for other manufacturers to abandon their analog

roots. Digitally controlled oscillators on analog synths became standard with the Juno-60, but Roland, as did Korg, Oberheim, and Sequential, all persevered with analog instruments right up until 1986-87 when Roland and Sequential finally acknowledged the overriding benefits of a fully digital system.

Casio, who had only burst onto the keyboard scene *at all* in 1980 with an army of 'home keyboards,' were the first to follow Yamaha's lead, and in 1985 launched their CZ Series synths, which used a digital system not wholly unlike Yamaha's FM, called Phase Distortion, PD for short.

The problem with both FM and PD, and in fact almost every digital system produced to date, is complexity when it comes to programming (see p.101). However, the reason that digital synths have not only survived, but have flourished, is that the basic range and quality of sounds they can produce far exceeds that of analog models. And through a magical device known as MIDI, it's possible to extend those sounds almost infinitely.

DX7

CZ-1

Wasp Synth

From 1983 onwards the synthesizer market has concerned itself with three things: MIDI, price, and the slow move towards digital generation and manipulation of sounds.

EVERYTHING YOU WANTED TO KNOW ABOUT MIDI BUT WERE AFRAID TO ASK!

The Basic Idea

In plain English MIDI (Musical Instrument Digital Interface) is the name given to a set of electronic rules and regulations for sending information back and forth between pieces of musical equipment that are blessed with special 5-pin Din MIDI sockets.

At first such pieces of musical equipment were all keyboards. Nowadays you'll find MIDI on almost all drum machines, drum pads, and on specialized wind instruments and guitars. There are even 'pitch to MIDI' converters that offer MIDI control from a microphone signal, allowing vocalists to 'play' a synthesizer by singing the notes into a microphone!

Similarly MIDI is not just found on instruments. Few manufacturers would dare launch a signal processor without MIDI, all current sequencers use MIDI, and there is a growing selection of ancillary equipment blessed with MIDI such as amps, mixing desks and lights.

MIDI is all about control, allowing one instrument to control certain aspects of another's performance. This can take the form of simply 'slaving' two keyboards together so that when you play *one* you hear *both,* or it can allow, say, a keyboard to trigger drum machine voices, or it can simply ensure that rhythmic devices like drum machines and sequencers keep in time with each other. Further down the line MIDI can allow you to manipulate (by 'remote' control) certain more specific aspects of a linked instrument's performance, like patch changes, or whether sounds are to respond to touch sensitivity.

Unfortunately, but necessarily, precisely what MIDI can accomplish on any given instrument or groups of instrument is not a static affair.

An instrument that 'supports' MIDI as they say, does not have to implement every little scrap of inter-communicatory gobbledy-gook on offer; it can pick and choose. MIDI simply dictates that if you want to be able to communicate a certain piece of information, 'this is how you do it.'

Accordingly, some MIDI-blessed instruments allow you to get up to all manner of sophisticated interplay and others simply permit a level of communication no more complex or all-encompassing than a two into one 'Y' connector.

Precisely what each MIDI-blessed instrument has chosen to implement is normally contained in its MIDI Implementation Chart — a nasty, complicated-looking stew of ******s, Xs and Os to be found stuffed up the back of the instrument's Owner's Manual. More of this later.

> *"There are so many aspects to MIDI and to the ways you can use it, it's hard to describe it all in one lump statement. For instance, if you play something in real time, you can strap as many sounds as you want onto that keyboard, which is wonderful! If you can pick the right sounds to layer on top of each other — some of them have spikes, some of them have pillows, some of them have sheets, some of them have rays, and they all work together — by all means go ahead and put four or five synthesizers on top of each other and create an unheard-of sound. But you really have to exercise judgement. So I audition sounds before I put them together. And I know what sounds I like certain instruments for. I'll go to the MemoryMoog for this, and the Jupiter for that. So there is less experimentation as you go along, once you've learned the strong elements of each instrument.*
>
> *JAN HAMMER*

Why Do We Need MIDI?

We don't. MIDI is a luxury item. Amazingly enough, life did exist before MIDI and some people actually managed to produce good music without it. Beethoven and the Beatles spring to mind.

Though it's often easy to forget, MIDI was brought into this world to make life easier, as in: 'Wouldn't it be nice if I could connect up all my synths and hear them all at once,' or 'I wish there was some way to change patches on all my synths without having to physically press buttons on each in turn,' or 'Wouldn't it be great if I could control stage lighting effects from my guitar.' Well, none of the above are exactly essential to the furtherance of playing good music, but all are undeniably neat tricks to have up your sleeve, and all are now possible using suitably accomplished pieces of MIDI equipment.

How MIDI Came About

You don't really need to know how MIDI came about, but it's worth giving you this potted history since it illustrates some of the problems involved in creating a communication system that strides across all manufactual barriers — problems that have, somewhat inevitably, manifested themselves in the final specification of MIDI.

In the late '70s and early '80s many synth players, frustrated no doubt at the ghastly limitations inherent in available equipment, spent a lot of time mucking about with instruments in order to link them up and control one from another. Several manufacturers made life easy for the inveterate fiddler by providing communications sockets to allow their own equipment to 'talk' to each other: Yamaha had their Key Code interface, Roland their DCB, etc., etc. And, of course, many a monophonic synth sported CV and Gate sockets — CV being Control Voltage, which took care of pitch; and Gate, which governed timings, the *length* of a note.

MIDI is simply an agreed upon common language allowing all manner of seemingly unrelated instruments to control or be controlled by each other.

Laurie Anderson ▷

The trouble was that although many instruments worked to a one volt per octave standard, several did not. The result on connecting up certain different brands of synthesizer? Cacophony.

During the early 1980s several far-reaching concepts were being developed. Sequential took the world by storm by using recently available low-cost microprocessors in the design of their first synthesizer, the Prophet-5, and soon everyone was doing it: Oberheim responded with the OB-X, Roland with the Jupiter-8. Polyphonic synths became affordable, stable, and fun.

At about this time sequencers were making a comeback — again thanks to affordable microprocessors (Roland's CSQ-100 and 600 came out in November 1980) and drum machines, too, were being made better and cheaper than ever. With all this new gear floating about, the question of incompatability (so and so's sequencer won't work with so and so's synth) was getting to be a real drag. Roland President Ikutaroo Kakehashi moaned about it to Tom Oberheim in the Summer of 1981. In turn Oberheim mentioned it Sequential's President Dave Smith, who was fired by the idea of a universal interfacing system and resolved to do some work on such a project in the Autumn.

After a Heads of Company meeting in October that year, a loose form of common ground was agreed upon. There were sceptics of course. This system couldn't be expensive: 'Why should I spend money on a concept that allows people to use other equipment apart from mine' was a common gripe (hence the inexpensive 5-pin Din as opposed to an XLR connector for instance). 'I'm not going to tell everyone all our trade secrets' was another. If this common language was going to work then manufacturers had, to an extent, to spill their technological beans — be honest with each other. And then there was the question of verbal communication between Japanese and American companies. 'Mono? Oh I see, I thought you meant Mono as in monophonic synth.' Crazy, maybe, but true. But an agreement was finally reached in August 1983 in Japan and published as MIDI Specification 1.0.

This document, now widely available (and in fact reprinted in a worthy tome entitled "MIDI For Musicians" by Craig Anderton), sets out the rules and regulations for entry into the MIDI club. Taking into account the above you can then understand why so many aspects and applications of MIDI have been left open-ended. To tie up all the loose ends would severely restrict the manufacturers' freedom to experiment, and the choice of features on their products.

The MIDI Modes

The driving force behind the initial work on MIDI was the desire to hook up two synths, made by different manufacturers, so that they work in tandem. But it quickly became apparent that MIDI's applications could extend much further than this, and a number of levels, or 'modes' of operation, were formulated. Logically enough, these are now known as MIDI Modes. There are four of them.

The first of these is Omni Mode, also known as Mode 1, or *Omni On, Poly*. This was designed as a 'power up' mode, whereby when two instruments are first switched on and connected via MIDI cables, all common ground information channels would be open. All available information could be discussed. 'All' — Omni, as in the Latin *omnis* meaning 'all', OK?

But then what if you were connected up to more than one instrument, to a sequencer perhaps, or a drum machine? Things could go really crazy if there wasn't a provision for specifying precisely *who* you wanted to be connected to at any given moment. Enter Mode 3 — *Omni Off, Poly*. Omni *off*, goodbye 'all,' hello someone in particular.

In this mode you have at your disposal a sort of 16-channel messenger service. By matching up Channel Numbers you can then communicate with a specific piece (or pieces) of equipment in a multi MIDI set up. Think of it like CB radio, whereby you can communicate with a specific person (or persons) on a chosen frequency band.

So what happened to Mode 2? As I mentioned in 'How MIDI came about,' the English/Japanese language barrier was responsible

"Since the advent of MIDI I've spent less time trying to come up with really brand new sounds. Because there are only a few sounds that you like and that you have to make for yourself. And I still do those — homemade. But on the other hand there are banks and banks of sounds coming down the MIDI pipeline and all you have to do is audition all of them — it'll take a while! — and then you pick some and you can always edit and make them fit what you want to do."
JAN HAMMER

for a number of notable early problems and the need for the eventual appearance of Mode 2 appears to be one of them. When a 'mono' mode was first discussed some people took it to mean mono as in monophonic synth — one voice only — whereas others took it to mean mono as in one voice at a time, separately controllable. The distinction will become clearer in a moment.

To satisfy both parties, Mode 2 *Omni On, Mono* (though similar to Mode 1 in that all available information is communicated on all channels) can only respond monophonically. Play a chord on your controlling synth, and, in this mode, a connected instrument will 'play' one note only. This note can be the highest, lowest, or last note in the chord depending on the note priority of the said instrument. Personally, I find this mode of dubious value, but there we are.

On the other hand, the similarly named *Omni Off, Mono*, Mode 4 is extremely handy. This mode only really applies to instruments that can split up their voices, allowing them to pump out a number of different patches, or sounds, simultaneously. Each individual voice can now be assigned its own MIDI Channel number — a feature that becomes vitally important when it comes to using sequencers. You know, or must have known, the old problem: You have a nice new synth, you buy a nice new sequencer which can 'record' and 'playback' umpteen different 'tracks,' but . . . drat . . . all the tracks come whizzing back to you using the same patch. The choice then becomes umpteen different tracks of bass, or umpteen different tracks of brass, or whatever. In Mode 4 you can now make Track 1 a bass sound, Track 2 a string sound and

Jan Hammer

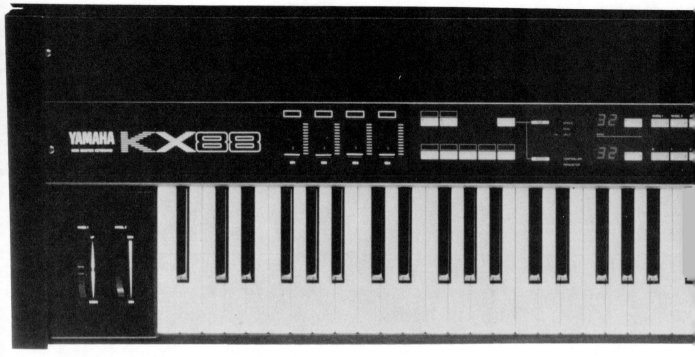

Yamaha KX-88

so on, thus creating a full and reasonably complete-sounding arrangement — still using just the one instrument.

Mode 4 has taken a while to get off the ground. For a while only Sequential seemed interested, then Oberheim joined in with the Xpander, and then Casio with their CZ range, but at last manufacturers seem to have caught on and there are a number of Mode 4-blessed instruments currently on the market.

But there are limitations. The MIDI spec has yet to tackle the thorny problem of who, how, and which detailed pieces of MIDI information get foisted onto which MIDI Channel.

As mentioned already, manufacturers can pick and choose what aspects of MIDI they put on their instruments, and this applies even to these basic modes. Some older models only included Mode 1, which means that even a fairly simple, Channel-assignable set up isn't even on. Most instruments do not implement Mode 4 because they do not have this 'multi-timbral' capability anyhow. Fortunately you can see at a glance precisely what an instrument *has* implemented by looking it up in its *MIDI Implementation Chart* under *Mode* — normally column number 2.

Channel Voice Messages

If I were writing a book on the subject, now would be the time to tell you about Channel Voice Messages and System Common Messages and the like. But I'm not, so I won't! Suffice it to say that MIDI can get extremely specific and detailed. You can, for example, decide to allow after-touch control over volume to be sent from your controlling keyboard, you can transfer program information from one synth to another, use personal computers, use MIDI to synchronize sequencers and drum machines, and so on. But the purpose of this chapter has been simply to introduce and explain only the basics of MIDI.

TYPES OF MIDI PRODUCT

Keyboards

1) The Master Keyboard

This can also be known as a Mother keyboard or MIDI Controller Keyboard. A true master keyboard contains no sound-producing circuitry of its own. Its job is to manipulate a number of MIDI-linked instruments and devices —

how each instrument 'appears' over the keyboard, sorting out split or layer points, remembering combinations, assigning different real time controllers like pitch and mod wheels, and generally masterminding an entire MIDI operation. Typical master keyboards include the Roland MKB-200, Yamaha KX-88, Akai MX-73, BIT Master keyboard.

2) The Remote Keyboard

This is similar to a master keyboard in that it cannot produce sounds on its own, but its main function is to operate as a roving or 'sling-on' type keyboard that can be strapped on like a guitar. Generally, Remote keyboards do not offer quite the same level of MIDI management as Master keyboards, but you should still be able to change patches, have separate access to more than one MIDI instrument, and be able to select and vary certain real time controllers. Typical models include the Roland Axis, Yamaha KX5, Korg RK-100, Casio AZ-1.

3) The MIDI Module

Nothing complicated going on here; a MIDI module is simply a keyboard-less instrument, which can be controlled either from a

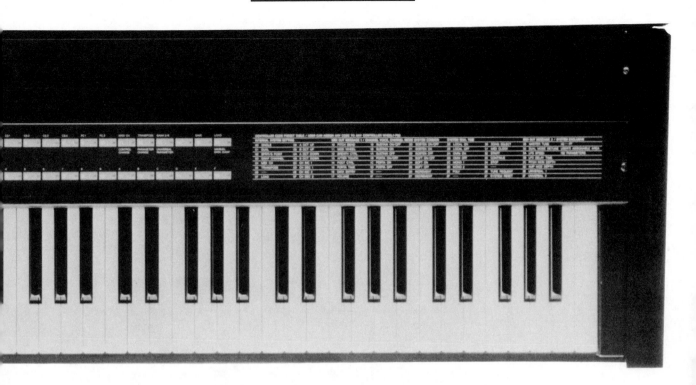

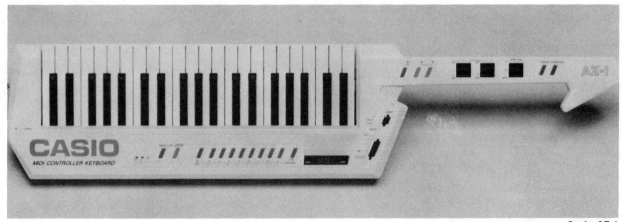

Casio AZ-1

Master keyboard, *any* other MIDI keyboard, MIDI drum pads, MIDI guitars. . . . . The beauty of modules is their lack of size and their cost-effectiveness. Since most of us only possess one pair of hands, to have umpteen *keyboards* littered about the stage/living room can simply be a waste of space and money. All types of instruments are now appearing in modular form: synths, pianos, samplers etc.

THINGS TO REMEMBER

MIDI can't do everything! If, for example, you hook up two synths, of which only one is touch sensitive, the non-touch sensitive one will always remain so. MIDI works on the 'common ground' principle. What might appear confusing, however, is the fact that several recent synths (the Yamaha DX21 for instance), although not blessed with their own touch sensitive keyboards, do have this capability built into their circuitry. In this case you can then make the instrument operate with player-controlled dynamics when a regular touch sensitive instrument is being used as a 'master' keyboard. Once again, this type of information can be found in an instrument's MIDI Implementation Chart.

George Duke with remote keyboard

Drums

1) Drum machines

MIDI is now standard on all drum machines. The reasons you will need MIDI controllability mainly concern sequencers — any make of which can so run in sync with any make of drum machine via the now always compatible MIDI clock. MIDI is also used when you want to 'play' drum machine sounds courtesy of an external controller. A controller can be a keyboard, whereby certain notes on the keyboard can be assigned to certain sounds on the drum machine, or it can be MIDI drum pads (see below) — any form of MIDI controlling device will do!

2) Drum Pads

A set of MIDI drum pads is the drummer's equivalent of a Master keyboard. They make no sounds, and are simply a way of triggering sounds contained in an external sound source — be it a MIDI synth, piano, sampler, whatever. By defining Note Numbers, you can 'tune' a series of pads to trigger specific notes on a MIDI instrument.

MIDI pads can also trigger sounds from a drum machine, of course, or 'effects' such as Tony Thompson's snare drum sound captured on a sampler! There are also several devices on the market that allow MIDI control from acoustic drums, via contact mikes and a box which converts the signal into MIDI pulses. (See p. 80 for further information on electronic drums and drum machines.)

Guitars

Roland have long championed guitar synths. Just as everyone thought that it was time to go home and give it up, the MIDI guitar seems, finally, to be taking off. MIDI guitar set-ups can either be complete units in themselves, as in Roland's still-burgeoning range, or comprise add-on units that can be fitted onto to your own guitar, along with a 'box' that converts the signal into controllable MIDI data (Roland allows this also). Newcomers include the Shadow GTM6 Guitar to MIDI system reviewed in these pages last month, the Synthaxe, and the Stepp DG1. (see p. 54 for more on guitar and bass synths).

GR-202

Also making great strides are 'pitch to MIDI' devices that convert audio signals into MIDI data. To an extent they are similar to drum triggering devices or MIDI guitar converters, but items such as the Fairlight Voice Tracker, or the IVL Pitchrider are (at least theoretically) suitable for controlling MIDI instruments (synths, pianos, drum machines) from, say, your voice or a woodwind instrument through a microphone. (see p. 16 for more on computers in music).

GUITAR SYNTHESIZERS

Guitar synthesizers of a sort have been around for some time. In the '60s, Vox brought out something called the 'organ guitar'; and in the early '70s, there was a kind of glorified synth effects unit called the 'Hi-Fly.' But these devices were always regarded as novelties by mainstream rock guitarists more interested in fuzz boxes and feedback. Until recently it looked as if guitars and synths could never be properly combined. And the main stumbling blocks revolved around the design and playability of the guitar in comparison to the keyboard.

Think of a keyboard. When you press down a key, it acts as a switch used to signal *note-on* information. Release the key, and it signals *note-off*. More recent developments have meant that you can signal a certain amount of touch and velocity sensitivity (see p. 18). Now think of a guitar. The strings are picked, plucked, stroked, strummed, damped, bent, hammered on, pulled off — and that's just in the first bar of the solo. You can see the problem. Guitarists have just too many ways of expressing themselves!

The first attempts at dedicated guitar synth design in the mid-'70s were monophonic, slow to respond and prone to mistrigger and 'glitching,' because they relied on a 'pitch to voltage' system whereby a special pickup 'read' string vibration and converted it into a signal voltage, giving note-on/note-off information. Guitarists remained sceptical. During the first half of the '80s, Roland produced the G 707 system and things began to

Signal Processors

Why do we need MIDI on a DDL? Once again I suppose we don't, but there are advantages, you know. By introducing a DDL or digital reverb into your MIDI set-up you can match individual settings to individual patches. You can set up a situation whereby on changing patches on your synth, a linked DDL will *automatically* change its

patch to a predetermined complementary setting. For live performances this capability should need no further justification.

MIDI and Personal Computers

Personal computers, such as the Atari 520ST, are now being produced with MIDI built in, but for a couple of years now one has been able to gain access to computer control via MIDI-Computer interfaces.

G-808

GR-505

"I've actually got a Roland guitar synth, and I've had to change my playing technique to use it. I'm normally such a sloppy player and because of the pitch-to-voltage system, every noise you make, every scratch on the strings, comes out. So instead of getting what should, in theory, be a nice sort of plucked DX7 sound or something, what you actually get is all these horrible noises belting out across the stage at the same level. So I ended up having to play with my hand so clear from the strings that it looked as if I'd broken my arm!"
MIDGE URE

look up. It was polyphonic and had access to a relatively wide range of sounds from its own synthesizer housed in a separate floor unit. (Its sister instrument, the GR 77B *bass* synth, is dealt with on p. 55 ; aside from the number of strings, the two are virtually identical). The Roland system was still not free of gremlins, however, and was difficult to play live.

Recently, however, there has been considerable improvement in the design of 'pitch-reading' models, and this is due mainly to the

development of digital synthesis together with the advent of MIDI. You can now choose between a dedicated system like the Roland, or a non-dedicated pickup and MIDI converter — like the Ibanez MC1 or Shado/Charvel GTM6 — which can be attached to *any* guitar and used to drive an external synthesizer.

Synthesized music is no longer the exclusive property of *keyboard* players. Through the wonders of digital technology, guitarists, bass players, and even drummers can now get access to an almost unlimited range of sounds. And this, in its turn, is bringing changes in the traditional role of these instruments in rock and the way in which they're played.

Perhaps more importantly, MIDI and the microchip have helped to create a new, and some would say revolutionary, type of dedicated guitar synth controller which uses *two* separate sets of strings: one to control note-on/note-off and velocity data; the other to trigger 'active' frets, which detect when a string makes contact with the fingerboard and convert this information into pitch and expression data. The leading designs in this field are currently the SynthAxe and the Stepp DG1.

G 707

The Two Systems Compared

Let's take the Roland GM70 as an example of the digital pitch-to-string approach. The latest system consists of the GK1 'hex' pickup and a small control unit, both of which will fit onto almost any standard electric guitar. These are then linked by a special lead to the GM70, a slim rack-mounted unit containing a 16-bit microcomputer. It has a sophisticated MIDI-OUT section allowing different combinations of strings to be linked up to different synths or synth voices. For example, the bottom four strings could have an orchestral string sound and the top two strings a flute-like sound.

The great advantage of this system is that it enables you to play the sounds of any MIDI-compatible synth from your favorite guitar. Also, as the sound of your guitar can be mixed in at any stage; you can change from, say, a rhythmic synth part to a bluesy guitar solo at the touch of a button. Furthermore, if you link this unit up to a synth that can receive the Omni-Off, Mono mode (see p. 44) you can send a signal from each string on six MIDI channels so that you can bend or use the tremolo arm on two or more strings at once without any problem.

So far so good. But now here's the bad news. There is a short *delay* between the time you pick the string and the time you hear the synth sound. This is because the guitar synth has to wait for the string to settle and then to follow one or two cycles of the waveform in order to convert the string pitch to digital code. This delay is more pronounced on lower notes, averaging at about 38 milliseconds. You won't notice it playing slowly, but it may hinder you when playing very fast runs. If you mix in some 'guitar' sound this will help mask the delay, but it does take a bit of getting used to (see p.107 for delay on bass synths and playing ideas for getting around this).

Roland GM70

GK1

The 'active fret' machines, meanwhile, are not really guitar synths as such. The SynthAxe, for example, makes no sound of its own; it was designed as a MIDI controller, a way of playing synthesizers using guitar techniques. The Stepp, on the other hand, is a kind of *electronic* guitar — a self-contained unit carrying its own onboard synth, but in no way functioning as a conventional electric guitar.

The big plus of these instruments is their lack of delay. Pitch is transmitted digitally by the strings on the neck making contact with the frets, while a completely separate set of strings act as note and velocity triggers. In practice this means you can play very fast and clean. You can isolate the neck strings — essential for two-handed fingerboard playing whether it be in the Stanley Jordan or Eddie Van Halen style! (See p.136.) The SynthAxe also features trigger

Stepp

BASS GUITAR SYNTHESIZERS

Introduction

HENRY: "Al, could you stop playing that piano for a moment?"

ALASTAIR: "That's not me, it's Geoff."

HENRY: "Are you crazy? That can't be Geoff!"

ALASTAIR: "No, honestly, I'm triggering the drums off the Akai sampler. Geoff's playing the piano off his Octapads."

GEOFF: "Wait a minute — so who's playing bass?"

DEIRDRE: "That's me, using the guitar synth."

HENRY: "Well, I'd better play with a steel drum patch, then!"

Background

In the history of synthesizers, the emergence of the bass guitar as a dedicated synth *controller* is very recent. In fact, the first usable sys-tem was only available from the end of 1983. Previously, for both analog and digital synthesis, the keyboard was the ideal interface — the keys acting merely as 'switches' to control the pitch, time and attack values of the signal voltage. In theory, however, a syn-thesizer interface can be *any* in-strument, as long as its sound can be converted into 'on' and 'off' pitch information that the synth's microprocessor understands.

Most dedicated guitar synth sys-tems have adopted a pitch-to-volt-age approach which relies on the interface (usually a special 'hex' pickup) being able to decide on the pitch of a string by reading its vi-bration. This has led to all kinds of problems for the player.

keys — six piano-style keys that can be played by the right hand. You can play them individually, or in groups of three or six for block chord effects.

So what are the drawbacks? Ex-pense. Neither instrument has a guitar sound of its own. The strings are all the same gauge and are divided into two separate sec-tions, which can cause problems of feel and expression when you're playing. As a guitarist, you will be used to string movement and ten-sion caused by what your *other*

hand is doing. The SynthAxe is quite heavy and bulky. The Stepp can only be played using a *metal* pick, so fingerstyle is out of the question.

Obviously, for some players the ideal would be a mixture of the ad-vantages of both these two sys-tems — i.e. an electric guitar with its own guitar sound, that could control synths without any delays. Unfortunately, such a system does not exist — yet. In the meantime, you have to pay your money and take your choice!

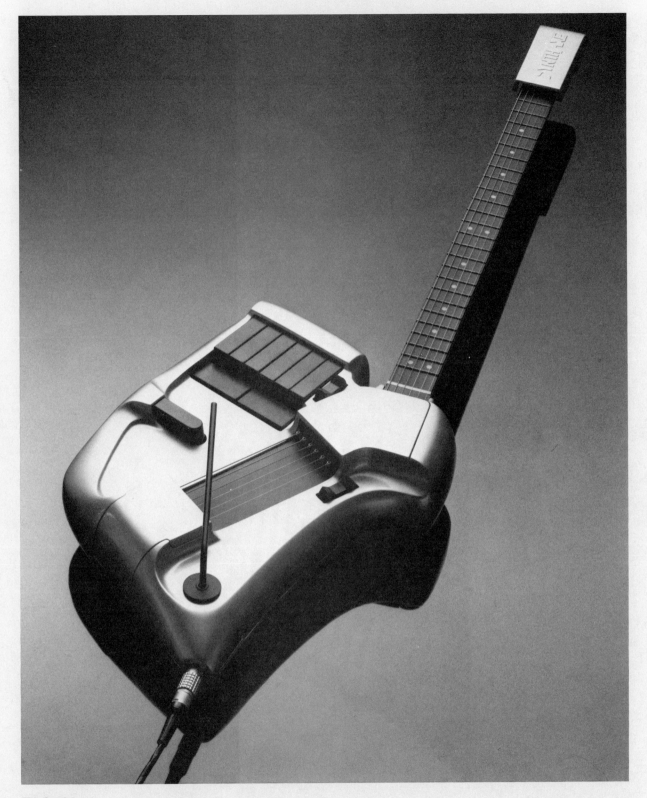

The SynthAxe

As it is now possible for guitar, bass and drums to trigger synth sounds, we are faced with the mind-boggling experience of not knowing who we are listening to at any one time, as was often the case during *ROCKSCHOOL* rehearsals. The existence of bass guitar synthesizer systems like the Roland GR 77B opens up endless opportunities to create sound textures, forcing us to constantly redefine the role of the bass player.

Henry with a G77 bass synth

When we talk about bass guitar synths, we're really talking about a bass designed to be used in conjunction with its own synthesizer or with other synths through MIDI.

To get around this, systems based on string-to-fret contact have been developed by SynthAxe and Stepp specifically for the lead guitar (see p. 54). But surprisingly, neither company has, as yet, a proposal for a bass guitar version. Bass players, meanwhile, have had to cope with the growing popularity of synth bass lines.

What most players and producers would love to see are more instruments that combine the playability and expressiveness of the bass guitar with the flexibility offered by synth sounds.

Roland Bass Guitar Synths

Roland orginally led the way in dedicated bass guitar synth controllers with the JX3P floor unit connected by a slightly awkward 24-pin adaptor plug and cable to either G88 or G33 basses fitted with hex pickups. As well as the normal tone and balance controls, these basses featured a touch plate for vibrato effects, a cut-off frequency pot, a mode switch, and balance controls for synth and 'ordinary' bass sounds.

By late 1985, Roland had developed an updated bass, the G77, which has the advantage of two humbucking pickups and speedier electronic circuitry. The most notable feature, however, is a stabilizing arm fitted between the body and headstock, designed to ensure greater accuracy of intonation and tone. This space-age guitar is also accompanied by a much more versatile floor unit, the JX8P. The whole set-up is called the GR 77B Bass Synthesizer.

The GR 77B has three outputs, two from the stereo synthesizer, and one from the bass guitar. Used simultaneously, you can get a quite staggering effect. Program change and editing can be carried out by the guitar controller and/or foot pedals. Creating new sounds is possible either by using an accessory programmer, the PG 800, or by editing on the floor unit, dumping or loading sounds via ROM cartridges. A unique feature of the GR 77B is its use of a separate microprocessor for each individual string, which makes for precise tracking, so keeping up with your playing ideas.

Henry's Live Set-Up

To keep pace with the sounds that Deirdre, Geoff and Alastair were coming up with at *ROCKSCHOOL* rehearsals, I had to get into slaving other synths and synth modules to my bass synth via MIDI. This in turn meant using a MIDI junction box (in this case the Quark MIDI-Link) to avoid the kind of time-delay gremlins you can encounter when you've chained together more than three synths at once via your MIDI THRU sockets. You can see the set-up I eventually assembled for the TV shows in the diagram below. It'll give you some idea of what you're up against if you want to match the kind of sounds made by the keyboard player in your band. *(See Fig. 23)*

The straight sound from the bass controller is sent to the volume pedal and from there it goes to an amp. This means that you now have independent control over your bass sound. The guitar output from the floor unit goes straight into an electronic tuner, so you can monitor and rectify any tuning problems instantly. The master volume still controls both the guitar and synth sound while the 'balance' pot only controls the synth sound. The synth can also be cut instantly by the mode switch.

The MIDI out of the floor unit goes into Channel 1 on the MIDI mixer. The slave units, in this case the Casio CZ 101 and Yamaha FB 101 module, are plugged into the output of the mixer via their MIDI sockets and are set to receive the signal from Channel 1, thus allowing all three synths plus the bass to play simultaneously. The final mix is blended with the effects, which are sent through an auxiliary 'send' and 'return' loop.

Since you are going to be dealing with synth sounds from such a system, you need to have full-range speakers that can handle the whole frequency spectrum. The output of the signal is fed from the mixer to the PA speakers via a stereo volume pedal so that you can balance the synths against the

G33 bass

bass guitar. If the individual sounds are not right on any one instrument, you are still able to change them physically because all the hardware is within your reach.

Don't expect to pick up a bass or guitar synth and instantly start playing "All Along The Watchtower" with an orchestra patch. You'll need to re-think your technique, phrasing and voicing with almost every new sound. But that's just part of the fun of synthesis! (For more on bass guitar synth programming and playing techniques, see p.107).

Power corrupts and bass players want a piece of it!

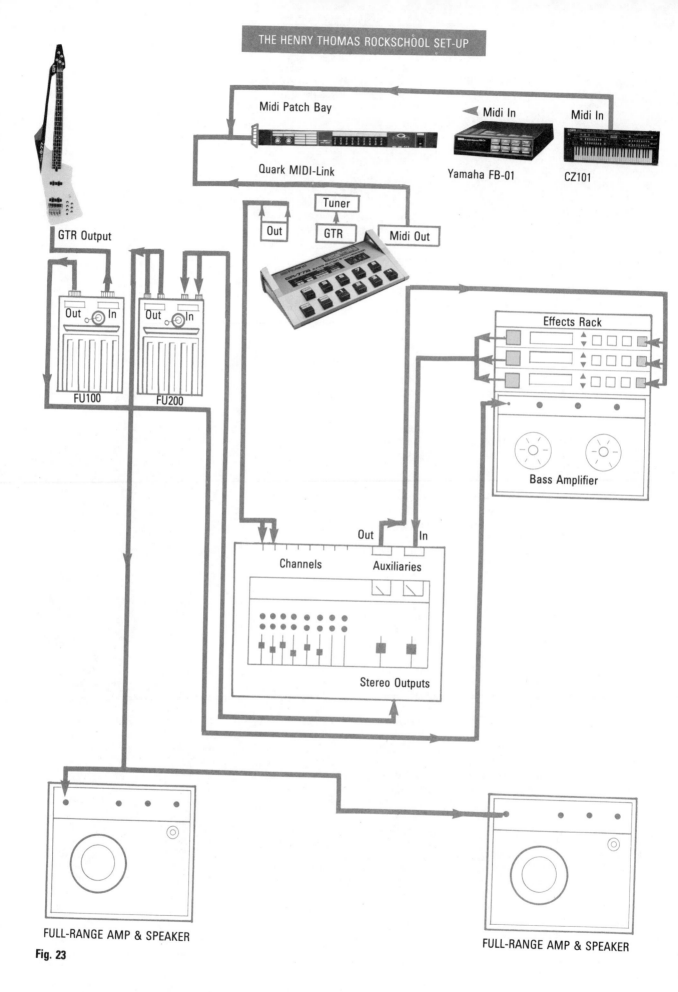

THE HENRY THOMAS ROCKSCHOOL SET-UP

Midi Patch Bay

Midi In

Midi In

Quark MIDI-Link

Yamaha FB-01

CZ101

GTR Output

Tuner

Out

GTR

Midi Out

Out   In

Out   In

Effects Rack

FU100

FU200

Bass Amplifier

Out   In

Channels

Auxiliaries

Stereo Outputs

FULL-RANGE AMP & SPEAKER

FULL-RANGE AMP & SPEAKER

Fig. 23

SEQUENCERS

A sequencer is a sort of tape re-corder, but with one vital differ-ence. It doesn't record *sound*. It records *information*. When it plays back, it instructs the synth to make the noises. This means you are not simply stuck with what you record into it. You can change things like timings, speeds, accuracy and sounds after the event, so to speak.

The appeal of sequencers is that they offer the musician freedom: not only freedom from one's own lack of dexterity in playing a key-board instrument, but also freedom from having to make up one's mind, irrevocably, as to how a per-formance should sound, as one does when recording onto a tape recorder.

Sequencers can be used with all instruments whose sounds are electronically generated (i.e., synths, electronic pianos, sam-plers, drum machines, etc.). You cannot sing into a sequencer, nor can you plug a normal electric gui-tar into it. A sequencer can be a free-standing 'instrument' in itself, it can be a piece of computer soft-ware (see p. 66), or it can simply be another feature you find built into a synthesizer.

Background

Although all manner of weird and wonderful contraptions for the 'au-tomatic' playing of musical instru-ments — music boxes, barrel organs, player pianos — have been developed since the early Middle Ages (the concept of letting some-one else's fingers do the walking is hardly new!) it wasn't until the early '70s that stand-alone boxes actually called sequencers arrived on the scene.

Most of the early models were analog devices, which required a fairly tedious form of programming involving separate commands for pitch, timbre, and timing instruc-tions. In those pre-MIDI days there was no standardized system for determining clock rates (see p. 42 MIDI) and should you cross the manufactual barrier, running say an Oberheim sequencer with a Ro-land synth, you were just asking for trouble.

As it happens, both Oberheim and Roland did a lot of pioneering work on sequencers, and though by today's standards such models as the Oberheim DS-2A (the first digital sequencer in fact) and Ro-land's MC-4 and MC-8 seem very

Roland's MC-4

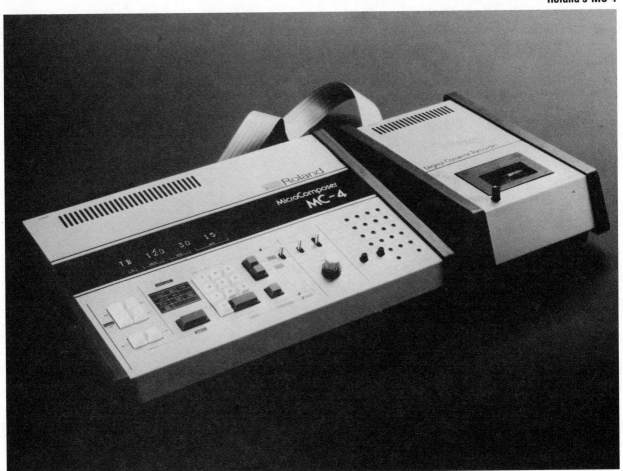

Sequencers can save you studio time and money. Instead of slaving over a hot multi-track tape re-corder laying down each part individually, you can program your sequencer, and when it comes to re-cording, lay the whole thing down at once.

Human League

Correctly programmed sequencers do not play out of time, they don't make mistakes and they don't get drunk or have rows with the management!

limited, they were regarded as state-of-the-art in their day (the distinctive sequencer part on the Human League's "Don't You Want Me?" was courtesy of an MC-4).

You normally think of a 'sequencer part' as just being a repetitive riff — as on "Don't You Want Me?" — or one of those glitteringly incessant synth parts so beloved of late '70s disco and hi-energy music. In the early days that was pretty well all a sequencer could do, since most were monophonic and only had a very small amount of memory. But in the early '80s, polyphonic sequencers began to appear, with the capacity to store *chords*, and accordingly the role of the sequencer began to change.

Once again Roland and Oberheim led the way, Roland with a series of CSQ and MSQ models, and Oberheim with the DSX. But until MIDI was developed polyphonic sequencers still had the problem of synchronization. Today, however, almost all the sequencers you'll come across will be digital, polyphonic, and will sport MIDI, which will allow them to control any connected MIDI synth or sound module, and play in time with any MIDI drum machine, relatively painlessly. The combination of polyphony and MIDI has meant that present day sequencers are no longer used simply to produce metronomically accurate little riffs, but can be used as cost-effective substitutes for multi-track recording facilities, and, dare I say it, musicians.

That said, there is still a wide variety of sequencers on the market and, seeing as the sequencer's main purpose is to make life easier, it is very important to examine carefully the level of 'sequencer power' you really need. Buying too sophisticated a model for your needs or skill will create far more problems than it solves.

Sequencer Uses

1. A sequencer can store one or more complete performances, 're-playing' them back to you on a whole range of different instruments or instrument programs. In other words your performance can be stored forever, but you can constantly update or improve the *sound* of that performance.
2. It can improve your performance by what is called *quantizing* or *auto-correcting* it — i.e., ironing out all the little timing discrepancies — to a number of specified accuracy levels.
3. It can *speed up* or slow down a performance without affecting pitch.
4. It can transpose a performance into another key.
5. It can play passages that you would find impossible (too fast, too complex).
6. In an overall sense, a sequencer can save you a vast amount of time and money when recording since keyboard and/or bass parts can be 'written in' at home and then replayed — completely accurately — with the push of a button once you get into the studio.

THINGS TO REMEMBER

1. A sequencer does not produce sound. It produces information about sound, which is then passed on to your connected instrument(s).
2. A sequencer will not allow you to do things that you couldn't (theoretically, at least) do with your connected instrument(s) alone. In other words if you try to play back an eight-note chord using a instrument that can only play six notes at a time, then bad luck! You will only hear six notes. Similarly, if you connect an instrument that can only play one sound across its keyboard (no key split or multi-timbral capability) then no matter how many individual 'tracks' there appear to be on your sequencer, all the tracks will play back on the same sound (eight tracks of bass, etc., not terribly helpful!). This problem can be overcome by connecting a sequencer to several instruments at a time, or by connecting one instrument that allows you to harness several sounds at a time (such as a Casio CZ-101, for instance).
3. Beware of older 'bargain' non-MIDI sequencers. You may find that they will not function properly with new synths, or with synths made by other manufacturers.
4. No matter what the publicity blurb says, all you will invariably want to do with a sequencer is store a few parts into it, hear what you played, played *better*, and be able to run the sequence in time with drum machines, and/or in time with the rest of the band in a recording studio. You will probably *not* want to spend hours altering the sustain pedal information on one note of a chord you inadvertently played in the middle of the last chorus. And thus bearing in mind that the more facilities a sequencer offers the more difficult it is to program and the more things there are to go wrong — be sensible about which sequencer you buy.

SEQUENCERS CAN BE A REAL HEADACHE!

Vince Clark

"I've worked with a lot of session musicians who simply can't play in time. I don't mean that horribly. When you're with a real drummer and a real bass player and everyone feels together, then OK. But in this situation, when you're working with a drum machine and it's got no mercy as far as timing's concerned, you know, the thing's got to be exactly right. And I like that style anyway. I like things to be metronomic and precise and exact, and I let Andy (Bell, vocalist with Erasure) do all the soulful bit, and put the feeling across in the song."

VINCE CLARKE

Korg SQD 1

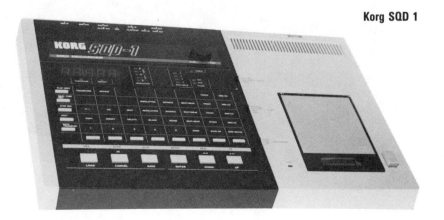

Andy Bell

A sequencer that offers no quantizing at all is about as useful as a guitar without strings on it.

"Usually our songs are written without any drum machines or synthesizers or anything being involved. Andy (Bell, vocalist with Erasure) and I sit at home with a piano or acoustic guitar and strum out a few chords. But we wouldn't go near any synths because it's too tempting to change the sound and that takes your mind off the songwriting process. So we just get the basic melody, record that onto a Walkman and bring it into the studio to write the accompaniment. We start off working out a bass line, then a drum pattern, developing a feel, a rhythm. Then we starting adding lines, building layers up, and that's where sequencing comes in."
VINCE CLARKE

Features to Look For

1. Ease of operation: You can't imagine how fed up you'll get with a sequencer that is a hassle to understand or use.

2. Multi-tracking capability: This can be offered either with dedicated 'tracks' or channels, or via MIDI, in which case each 'track' is specified simply by being on a particular MIDI channel number. You will probably want the option of recording on at least six tracks, though most current MIDI sequences do now offer at least 16!

3. Quantizing options: In practice you will use three or four types of quantizing: Off — in other words leaving your timings intact; 8th note — whereby the sequencer will be quite severe on your playing and not replay any notes 'in between' eight beats to the bar; 16th note — not so severe; and 32nd note — fairly forgiving! Triplet variables of these are also useful options.

4. Editing: Detailed editing capabilities are useful up to a point. Undoubtedly it is helpful to be able to correct one or two notes rather than re-record an entire sequence, and it also helps if a sequencer can either accept or ignore certain things like velocity sensitivity. However, editing features can make a sequencer fiddly and overstretched in terms of memory — especially on personal computer-based sequencer software.

5. Sync options: Rarely will you use just a sequencer and a synth. Normally you will want to play in time with drum machines (see p.113), and, in a recording studio, you may want to record a sequencer part onto an already recorded piece of music. In the first instance all pieces of rhythm-based MIDI equipment like sequencers and drum machines will play in tandem quite naturally over MIDI because MIDI has a standard clock rate. In a studio situation, however, things may not be quite so simple, and you may have to deal with special synchronization systems like SMPTE and FSK. And then there's the problem of older, non-MIDI equipment too. Although it is not practical to expect a sequencer to offer a complete range of 'sync' options, basically, the more the merrier!

6. Step-time/Real-time programming: Precisely what these mean is covered on p.113, but always look for both options on a sequencer.

7. Memory: This is basically how much information the sequencer can hold at any one time, and is normally measured in terms of *event memory*. An event is any type of command, be it about notes, pitch benders, velocity sensitivity or whatever. A sequencer with a 30,000 event memory is by no means excessive, especially when recording playing characteristics like velocity, which guzzles up memory space at an unbelievable rate. Many sequencers now offer the option of off-loading data onto discs — a feature well worth looking out for.

9. Song pointers: Not all MIDI sequencers respond to the song position pointer, but this is an extremely valuable attribute to have. Sequencers and drum machines that have implemented this feature can both lock into a particular part of a song without one of them having to be reset. In other words if you want to practice, say, a line over the second chorus, you can start your drum machine at the relevant bar and the sequencer will immediately begin playing from the same place.

SEQUENCER TYPES

1. Dedicated.

A dedicated sequencer is a sequencer that is a sequencer and nothing else. Normally they are free-standing units that only require power, and connections to and from your keyboard(s), in order to function. Generally they are easy to use, but offer little in the way of visible help when it comes to detailed editing (as a rule they have very small display screens). A dedicated sequencer is normally replaced by a newer model rather than updated, whereas personal computer sequencing software can always (in theory) be updated by the manufacturer for little or no extra money on your part. See below. A second-hand dedicated sequencer is not a particularly good bet — for the buyer or seller!

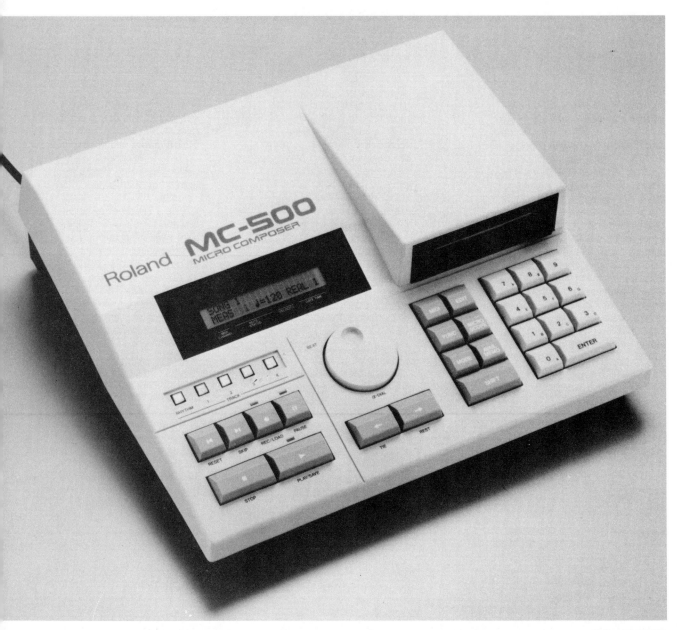

Roland MC 500

*Examples: Roland MC 500
Yamaha QX5
Korg SQD-8

2. Personal computer software.

Sequencing programs have been written for all the major personal computers, notably for Commodore, Apple, Apple Maccintosh, Spectrum, BBC, and Atari. While the standard varies considerably from program to program, few are exactly simple to use; most require at least some knowledge of computers *whatever* the manufacturers might claim to the contrary.

However, should you already own a PC, then this is certainly the cheapest way of obtaining real sequencing power, as the programs themselves are relatively inexpensive. For a number of reasons (computer memory, large screen display, updatable capability) PC software sequencing can be the most challenging and rewarding. It can also be the most frustrating. (For more on computers and music, see p. 68).

*Examples: Hybrid Arts (various)
Atari ST
UMI-3S BBC
Steinberg Pro 16/24
Atari ST
C-Lab Supertrack
Commodore

3) Synths with built-in sequencers.

I wouldn't recommend buying a synth solely because it has a built-in sequencer, but it might well tip the balance in its favor. Most built-in sequencers offer only one or two tracks of recording and normally have a very small amount of memory. However, if all you want to accomplish is the odd repetitive riff or tightly played synth bass line, then this may be quite sufficient.

*Examples: Ensoniq ESQ-1
Roland JX3P/JX-10

Ensoniq ESQ-1

JX-10

COMPUTERS IN MUSIC

Many musicians feel that computers have no place in music. Well, unless you've restricted your keyboard playing to Hammond organs or acoustic pianos for the past five years or so, you've been at the mercy of computers for quite some time now.

Almost all modern keyboards function thanks to microprocessors (minute electronic circuits embalmed in slivers of silicon) which are, in effect, hidden brains that control almost their every move.

So why be frightened of computers?

No reason, really, except that to use computers in music may take a bit of getting used to, learning a few bits of jargon here, developing a bit more patience there. But in the end, not to attempt to understand how or why computers can help the creation and organizing of music is to miss out on a whole range of facilities that are simply not available elsewhere. And to miss out on a lot of fun!

When we talk of computers in music there are in fact two distinct types of computer to choose from: a dedicated music computer, and a personal computer run with music software.

Dedicated music computers

A dedicated music computer is one designed specifically for musical applications. The Fairlight, Synclavier, and Yamaha CX5 are probably the best known examples.

The Fairlight comes from Australia (*see Sampling, p.*103). It is not cheap (about $100,000!) and is undoubtedly one of the most advanced musical instruments ever made. Not only can it re-produce built-in sounds, but you can create your own sounds using advanced forms of digital synthesis, sample sounds, and write long and complex sequences.

"I think that for people who can't necessarily play, who haven't spent years studying guitar or whatever instrument or technique, but have got good songs and good lyrics and want to put those ideas across, then I think computers are great for those people. It means they can translate their ideas straight away."

VINCE CLARKE

The "Art of Noise" with a computer

Computer music/computers *in* music. Don't confuse the two. Choosing a computer to help you make music has little or nothing to do with computer music. Computer music is a style of writing and production based upon metronomic rhythm and electronic sounds. Simply using computers to help you organize and/or store your music will not suddenly make you sound like Kraftwerk or Thomas Dolby!

Synclavier

The same description would also fit New England Digital's Synclavier (aside from the price — which you can double!). In fact both are really better described as complete work stations rather than instruments, especially the Synclavier, which allots a vast amount of power to multi-track recording. Frank Zappa's "Jazz From Hell" album is, aside from one track, entirely written, performed, and 'recorded' on a Synclavier. As for the Fairlight, it would be quicker to enumerate those who haven't used one — though not in so complete a sense.

The Yamaha CX5 (latest model CX5M11/128) is a little more down to earth. Based on the MSX format — a Japanese favorite that has failed to impress many other countries to date, the CX5 contains a number of editable sounds and a small sequencing section.

But although the CX5 was designed specifically for music applications, it can also take advantage of any other (musical or non-musical) MSX software that you might have available. In this respect it veers towards the second, and by far the most common, form of computer use in music: that involving the personal computer.

Personal Computers

A personal computer is entirely dependent upon *software*, a set of instructions stored either on disks or tapes, to tell it how to behave. The same Commodore 64 can therefore be a telephone directory one

minute, an accounting system the next, then a word processor, and after that, a 16-track digital recording studio.

Music-oriented software for personal computers started being written shortly after personal computers themselves arrived on the scene in the late '70s; the Apple, and (by 1981) the Sinclair ZX81 being the two most popular choices of aspiring music software writers.

For the first couple of years most music software was not very attractive: fun for computer buffs, tedious for musicians. Although pundits were quick to pounce on it as *the next big thing,* even in 1987 this has failed to happen. Although few people would now doubt that computers hold the key to the fu-

---

To use computers in music you do need to understand a little about computers. To learn all you'll need is not nearly as difficult as you think.

Frank Zappa

computer interfaces that allowed music software to control sounds produced by regular synthesizers.

Unfortunately, computer manufacturers have no standard language like MIDI, so for each brand of computer one needs a special interface in order to link up with MIDI instruments. It's no bad thing, therefore, that MIDI interfaces are relatively inexpensive.

Although interfaces for most of the major personal computers (Commodore, BBC, Spectrum, Apple, and Apple MacIntosh) continue to be made, a new breed of computer has come on the market since 1986: a computer already blessed with MIDI terminals, the most visible at present being the Atari 520ST and 1040ST.

Uses

Why do we need computers in music? We don't, any more than we need MIDI, digital recording, sequencers, or any of the other computer-based gadgets and concepts that increasingly have taken over the average music shop during the past few years. But, believe it or not, like the rest of the list, computers are on offer to make life easier.

Sequencing (see p. 65): This is one of the computer's most widely used applications. The practicality of sequencing software varies enormously from computer to computer and from software to software, encompassing anything from simple one or two track step time packages up to 24-track programs which allow precise and detailed examination of your every move.

"You know what a compact disc is? It's a sample! There actually isn't any real music on it, just a series of numbers that have been assigned to the different parameters of the music. And when you play the disc, the player actually decodes the numbers into electrical impulses which in turn get sent to your amp and speakers and come out as music. Well, top grade samplers like the Fairlight or E-Mu can sample with the same fidelity as a CD. We can now sample or digitally record true natural sounds or acoustic instrument sounds, play them from the digital instrument and what you really hear is a trumpet or piano or voice, and it sounds like the real thing. Just like a record sounds like the real thing."

HERBIE HANCOCK

ture of music-making, precisely when this future will come to be realized is far from certain. Music software continues to grow in range, application, and user-friendliness, and musicians are slowly beginning to lose their in-built fear of computers.

Much of the early software was centered around computers' own sound-producing capabilities. Until the Commodore 64 came along (with its famous SID chip — Sound

Interface Device), offering polyphony and a reasonable crop of sound editing facilities, the fact that most computers' sound chips had been designed purely for computer-games' 'winning/losing' fanfares meant that the results of one's labors still *sounded* rather cheap and nasty.

The situation improved dramatically after the adoption of MIDI, when a number of small companies began producing MIDI-

Herbie Hancock

Mike Pinder

There are several advantages in using a computer sequencing program instead of a dedicated sequencer:

1. Price — provided you already own a computer and monitor screen the actual cost of the software will be far less than the dedicated hardware equivalent (the Atari Pro-24 costs around $500).

2. Control — armed with computer power you can generally delve far deeper into sequences, altering individual note volumes, lengths, notes themselves, pedal information, etc.

3. Visibility — no dedicated sequencer can compete with a computer monitor screen when it comes to displaying information.

4. Updates — while it can be madly irritating to have to wait for some rumored update to improve your sequencer to come through, at least such an entity exists. A sequencer program can then easily be updated and improved as the manufacturer improves its design. If you buy a dedicated sequencer, what you buy is generally what you're stuck with for life.

Patch editing and storing: A computer can be used to help you program your instrument. Most synths and samplers carry as few movable controls as possible and generally sport tiny display screens. On a computer monitor much more information can be shown. This is especially helpful on sampling instruments, where such things as finding looping points can be murderously difficult without any decent visual aid.

Alongside editing programs (one piece of software tackling one instrument at a time, i.e., DX7 Editors, etc.) you will often find a large chunk of memory for storing patches, voice library. Sounds can then be stored externally, on disk or casette, which in effect makes your instrument unlimited in patch storage terms.

Although software for sequencing, instrument editing, and voice libraries make up the vast majority of current music software, programs are also available for sampling, effects (DDLs, echoes, etc.), MIDI management, and music writing (scorewriters).

SAMPLERS

Sampling, the business of capturing a sound on some form of storage and retrieval system and then re-triggering it, today normally from a keyboard, can be traced back to the 1950s, to *musique concrete*. It became fashionable to record (normally on tape) *real sounds*, then cut them up and re-use them, out of context as it were, as part of a performance. Performance being the operative word, it was inevitably rather a hit and miss affair.

The first time such a concept was used on a marketable instrument was in the early '60s, when a British company called Streetly Electronics produced an outrageous beast called the Mellotron. Mellotrons stored sounds on banks of pre-recorded ³/₈ inch tape. You press a key, the appropriate pitch of the sound whirrs past the tape replay head and hey, presto!

Mellotrons were notoriously unreliable, however, and relatively few people could afford to bother with them. Bands such as Genesis, King Crimson, Barclay James Harvest, and the Moody Blues (whose keyboard player, Mike Pinder, worked for Streetly in the early days) were all regular users,

though. The Beatles used a Mellotron for the flute sounds on ''Strawberry Fields.''

Although Streetly Electronics only went out of business last year, Mellotrons ceased to be of any lasting value in the '70s. And it wasn't until 1979 that *digital* sampling, as we know it today, was first seen on another instrument. That instrument was the Fairlight from Australia.

The Fairlight is much more than just a sampler, however. It is a dedicated music computer that can be used as a powerful sequencer, as a digital sound creator, and editor. But it was the sampling side of things that caught the eye of a young synth designer from California named Dave Rossum. To him this was *the feature* on the Fairlight. Why bother with all the rest?

Rossum's company, E-Mu, had been building large, analog, modular synthesizers for a number of years. Fired by what he'd seen on the Fairlight, he set about producing a dedicated sampler — an instrument whose sole purpose was that of recording and replaying sampled sounds.

It only took less than a year for Rossum to produce the Emulator, and though only capable of sampling for two seconds, the instru-

ment caused quite a ripple of excitement upon its launch in 1980. Excitement among players, yes, but few manufacturers deemed it worth investigating as yet. And it is amazing that by the time the highly successful E-II came out in 1984, hardly anyone else had bothered to produce a rival during the intervening years.

With the E-Mu E-II things really got moving. The instrument was immediately responsible for a severe outbreak of 'sampling fever.' Who *didn't* use the famous 'Orchestra Stabs' (originating from the Fairlight, in fact) on their record in 1984?

For a while sampling instruments were of interest almost solely to American manufacturers. New England Digital, makers of the giant Synclavier, took it up, then Kurzweil, a new company who'd managed to persuade Bob Moog onto the payroll, then Ensoniq — another new company formed by Ex-Commodore computer personnel, and Electro-Harmonix out of New York, who enjoyed reasonable success with their non-keyboarded Replay machine. And it was on this design that Akai, the first of the Japanese companies to investigate sampling, based their S612.

E-MU&E-11

WHAT YOU WILL NEED

a) A computer
b) A disk drive (unless one is built-in, or your computer uses cassette storage)
c) A monitor
d) A MIDI-computer interface (unless MIDI is built-in)
e) Software

"The Mellotron was a notorious instrument. The early one I had was a great big thing made out of whatever they could lay their hands on — bicycle chains, vacuum cleaner motors. They had these ridiculous drums with tape on them and you had to search these tapes to find the tone you wanted — and the whole system just went wrong all the time. We got to the stage where we were rebuilding it every night because it was structurally so unsound. It was real chaos"
TONY BANKS

"I do use a little bit of sampling for drum sounds and percussion. But generally I've gone off it a bit. I mean, I did it for about two years with the Fairlight and I think it's been used too much. Once you've sampled a sound it's very difficult to alter it. Whereas you can go to one of the older analog synths, twiddle the knobs, and you'll get something that nobody else in the world would get, and something that you'd never get again. So it makes it more original and more interesting."
VINCE CLARKE

Paul Hardcastle

By now the race was on to make a high quality but low cost sampler that could be used as a replacement for mid-quality polyphonic synths. Ensoniq did very well with the Mirage, soon followed by Sequential with the Prophet 2000, and in 1986 the full weight of the Japanese was felt when Roland, Korg, Akai, and ultimately Casio (though with an extremely low cost, home keyboard model) all took the plunge.

To date Yamaha remains notable by its absence, save for a Casio-type home keyboard version, though it is rumored that a profes-

sional Yamaha sampler will arrive soon!

The current state of the sampler market is healthy, but cautious. User-sampling has yet to be made anything like foolproof, and most people prefer to wade through stacks of factory disks or customized disks for the majority of their sounds. In other words the instruments might just as well be preset ones. Quite silly in a way.

The danger, of course, is that if everyone insists on sticking to library disks then the whole point of sampling — having the ability to pluck your own sounds out of the sky — is rather lost. Few people

bother to use samplers creatively. Paul Hardcastle n-n-n-n-n-Nineteen-ing his way to the top of the charts barely even scratches the surface of what is possible.

In as much as a synthesizer, thanks to MIDI, doesn't have to sport a keyboard these days, neither do samplers, and many companies are now offering the module-of-the-sampler as a lower-cost option. Sampling can also be undertaken on personal computers, and there are a number of excellent pieces of sampling software on the market for all the major computers.

DRUMS AND ELECTRONICS

Introduction

Of the four instruments basic to rock music — guitar, bass guitar, keyboards and drums — the drums were the last to go electric. Electric guitar and bass are synonymous with rock, of course, while keyboard synths have either ousted the acoustic piano or at least added greatly to the keyboard player's range.

It remains to be seen whether acoustic drums will go the way of acoustic piano. But certainly there is an increasing live use of electronic pads, while in the studio, drum machines, samplers and sequencers are used as much or even more than acoustic kits.

This revolution has taken place in a remarkably short period. Although drum machines have been around for some time, it was the introduction of the Linn LM-1 in the late '70s that launched the first serious challenge to the acoustic drum.

The electronic kit, meanwhile, is a true child of the '80s, pioneered by the British company Simmons Electronics.

Electronic Drum Kits

Dave Simmons is a keyboard player who, in the late '70s, experimented with analog synth modules played via drum pads. The electronics were similar to those used in analog keyboards, but concentrated on the percussive elements of the sound. The first commer-

Simmons Electronic Drum Kit

cially marketed unit was the SDS 3 drum *synthesizer*, closely followed in 1980 by the hugely successful SDS 5 electronic *kit* with its distinctive hexagonal pads.

These pads had a relatively hard polycarbonate surface beneath which transducer 'piezo' pick-ups transmitted the timing and approximate force of the players' strokes to the 'brain' of the kit. Here the sound is generated and put out to an amplifier.

The hard playing surface has been the cause of major criticism, since drummers unwittingly came to strike the pads with too much force, causing wrist fatigue and worse. The other major criticism is the lack of touch sensitivity and dynamics as compared with the acoustic drum.

Along with expanding the range of available sounds, Simmons have concentrated on improving the playability of their pads. They have been closely followed by their competitors, of course. Pads now tend to have rubberized playing surfaces (Simmons, Dynacord, Roland, Yamaha, Pearl, *et al*), or real drum heads tensioned over foam pads (D-drum, Tama, Sonor). Yet even with real heads, because of the need for a foam underlay, the feel is not identical with that of an acoustic drum. But the relatively uniform and firm playing surfaces actually make certain aspects of playing easier than on acoustic drums.

Touch sensitivity is getting better all the time. It's now possible to achieve something approaching a soft closed-roll on certain of the electronic kits. Dynacord have devised a system where alternate strokes trigger a dual sound source so that beats merge into one another during fast rolls, as they do when played on acoustic drums. This is an improvement on the 'machine gun' discrete effect characteristic of most electronic kits and drum machines.

Another aspect of touch sensitivity is the fact that real drums and cymbals have different tonal and playing characteristics over their entire surface. A normal electronic pad with a single trigger pick-up cannot mirror this expressiveness. Simmons are consequently introducing 'zone intelligent' pads with their SDX system, which sense both how hard and *where* they are struck.

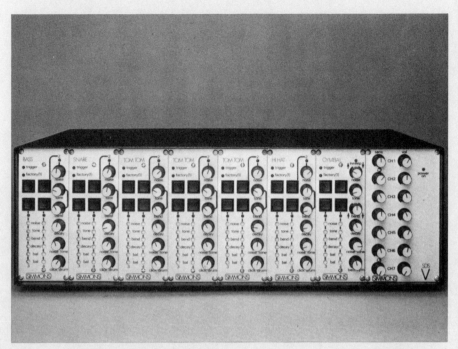

SDS 5

SDSV

Sound

But it hasn't always been like this. The SDS 5 was an entirely analog synthesizer. The components of its sound were simply a tone, some filtered white noise, and a 'click' to provide the initial impact. With pitch bend, the familiar "doom-doom" tom sound was produced. The 'snare drum' sound included a little extra noise for increased sibilance.

The problem was that this sound was so distinctive it was in danger of becoming a novelty. Consequently, the next step for Simmons and other manufacturers was to expand the range and quality of their sounds through increased

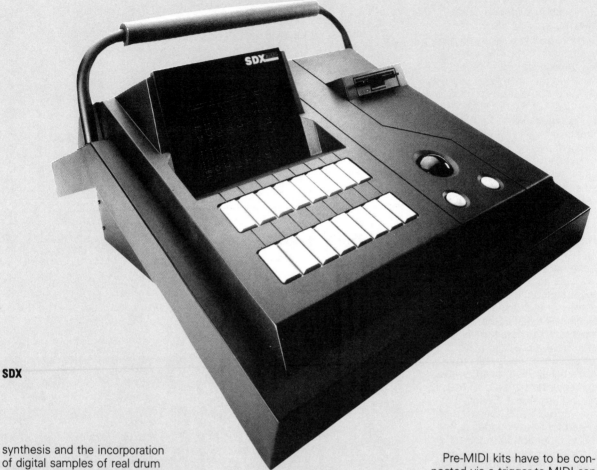

SDX

synthesis and the incorporation of digital samples of real drum sounds.

The SDS 7, therefore, combines analog and digital sound sources which can be edited and combined in varying degrees. Other manufacturers, including Roland and Dynacord, concentrate on digital-only systems, which offer great scope for editing and effects. Further variety is available through ever increasing ranges of sampled sounds, and user-samplers are already a part of Simmons and Dynacord systems.

MIDI Sound Expansion and Effects
Much of the technology and advantages of MIDI, which was originally developed for keyboard set-ups, has now been passed along to electronic drums and drum machines.

This means that drum pads can now be used to play other drum machines or synthesizers, for example, keyboard synths or expanders. The sounds from these instruments can be combined or layered, or accessed separately. The pads can also be played into a MIDI sequencer/recorder so that the real time performance can be encoded, edited and time-corrected without committing to tape. Alternatively, drum machines or keyboards can be made to trigger the sounds of electronic drum kits.

Pre-MIDI kits have to be connected via a trigger-to-MIDI converter (see diagram below), while recent kits have MIDI capability built in.

Powerful MIDI systems such as the Simmons SDS 7/MTM, the Dynacord ADD-1 and the Yamaha PMC-1 in combination with tuned synths, enable the drummer to go far beyond the accessing of multiple drum sounds. For example, with the Simmons set-up, the drummer can play *tuned* sequences or riffs, chords, glissandi and echoes, or build up chords under dynamic control with extra notes being added as the pad is struck harder. And with programmable re-routing, the bass drum can be assigned to a tom tom pad, and so on.

The great advantage of all electronic kits is the range of sounds which can be got from a single pad set up. Literally dozens of different kit configurations can be stored as patch or kit numbers, and sequences of such kits can be accessed for live performance with the help of a foot pedal or equivalent device.

"Percussionists have always been used to striking different surfaces, and I never subscribed to this argument that electronic drums should be the same as acoustic drums. The whole idea it seemed to me was that they should *not* be the same, and, in as much as the manufacturers kept trying to make them like acoustic drums — I wasn't interested. I like them because they are a different instrument and require a different attitude from the drummer."

BILL BRUFORD

Geoff playing acoustic/electronic drums

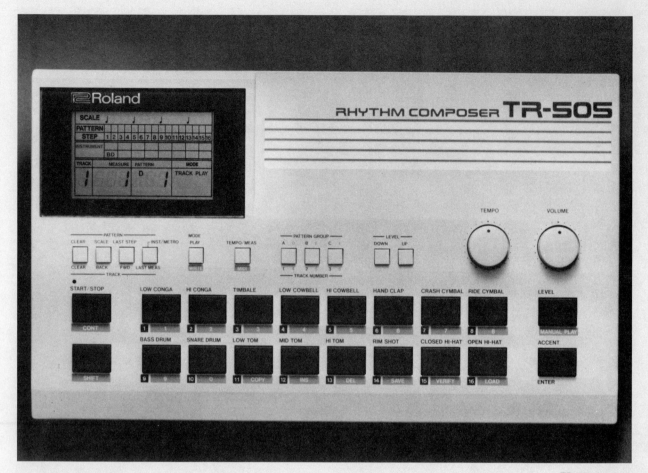

TR 505 for U.S.

Drum Machines

If Dave Simmons is synonymous with the history of electronic drum kits, Roger Linn holds an almost equivalent pride of place in the development of drum machines. Drum recording techniques were revolutionized when Linn incorporated high quality samples of real drums into his LM-1 design. Not only does the LM-1 have studio quality sounds (digitally recorded on EPROMs), but by using computer technology it enabled drum tracks to be built up convincingly enough on record to replace the performance of a real drummer.

The problem of the Linn sound becoming too familiar was forestalled by the introduction of a continually updated sample library of interchangeable sound chips. The LM-1 was succeeded by the (in)famous Linndrum, followed by the Linn 9000, which set another record by being the first drum machine to incorporate a multi-(32)-track MIDI sequencer.

All three Linn designs have been aimed at the top end of the professional market and as such have become industry standards. However, developments have been so rapid that machines in the middle and lower price ranges have already achieved a remarkable level of sophistication.

Digital 'real' sounds, whether PCM or EPROM-derived, have ousted analog sounds. On a mid-priced machine you can expect to alter the pitch, decay, and output of the sounds, and assign them to different key pads, as necessary. The pads themselves will be touch sensitive. The range of available sounds can be extended from a library of sound chips, ROM cards, cartridges, or disks. You can output the sounds in several different ways: straight mono or panned stereo (for stage monitoring or porta-studio mixing), or separate individual outs for multi-track mixing.

Cheaper units with great sounds are also now available, but with a number of drawbacks: less mem-ory, fewer sounds, no editing, and no individual outputs.

The Drummer as Complete Musician

The Linn 9000 was the first drum computer incorporating a multi-track MIDI sequencer, the Emulator SP-12 the first with user-sampling as standard. The new Sequential Studio 440 is a drum machine that samples *and* sequences, while the Simmons SDX is a conventionally playable electronic kit that will sample, record and edit sounds. Very fine tuning of samples, which can include pitched instruments such as bass guitar, vibes, timpani, etc., is possible with both the Sequential and the Yamaha RX5 drum computer.

These products are, or have been, at the forefront of R&D, but they suggest that in the not too distant future, all these aspects of playing, composing and recording will be conveniently and economically available to the drummer.

"As a drummer, I've always been interested not only in rhythm, but also in melody and harmony. And the new technology gives you control over those things. You can come to rehearsal with a large part of your composition worked out — not just the rhythm pattern. You can influence other musicians with your chords and shapes. You can be a real musician!"
BILL BRUFORD

Amplification

An advantage of drum machines and electronic kits is that they are relatively compact and portable. But for live work you'll still need hardware, perhaps a set of real cymbals, and, of course, amplification.

Monitor amplification for electronic drums is still in its infancy. Whereas guitar, bass and, to a lesser extent, keyboard amplification is now quite highly developed, drummers are faced with problems of frequency range, high volume and attack — all of which demand a very robust amplifier indeed!

EPROM = Erasable, Programmble, Read-Only Memory;
PCM = Pulse-Code Modulation;
ROM = Read-Only Memory.

However, there are a few reasonable dedicated drum amplifiers now available and they can only get better.

Drum and Drum Machines Set-Ups

An electronic drum kit usually consists of a set of pads that trigger the sounds generated by the kit 'brain.' If the pads are connected to a trigger-to-MIDI converter, or have this facility built-in, they can be used to play any MIDI drum machine or synthesizer. In other words, the pads can be used just as controllers with no specific dedicated sound source of their own.

The Roland Pad-8 Octapad is a simple but very versatile example. The eight pads of this single unit can be used to play four banks of eight sounds each. Each pad in each bank can be assigned a MIDI *note number*, which corresponds to the note on the tuned synth or voice of the drum computer you wish to play. All you need is a single MIDI lead. *(See Fig. 24)*

Fig. 24

OCTAPAD — Out — Midi — In — "SLAVE" SYNTH or DRUM MACH. ETC.

Octapad

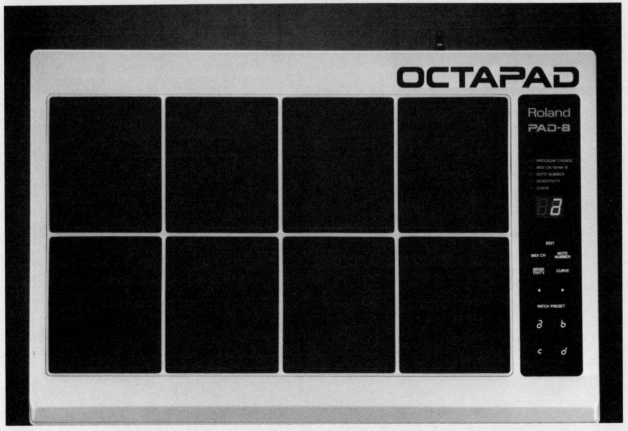

You may wish to play notes from the synth during one part of the performance and beats from a drum machine during another. To do this, you only have to connect another MIDI lead and assign a different MIDI *channel* (1 to 16 — see p. 44) to the synth and drum machine. *(See Fig. 25)*

The MIDI THRU connection ensures that the information at MIDI IN of the synth is passed to MIDI IN of the drum machine.

When Octapad and drum machine are both on channel 'B' in the diagram above, and the appropriate note numbers have been dialed up on each unit, the pad will trigger the drum sound you require, but not the tuned note corresponding to this MIDI note number on the synth. Of course, if the synth were set to Channel 'B' as well, you would hear both the drum voice *and* the synth note.

Furthermore, with some modern drum machines, such as the Korg DDDI or Yamaha RX 5, you can assign any MIDI note number to any drum voice you wish. In fact, you can assign the same note number to two or more sounds — say, snare and handclap. When you strike the right pad on the Octapad, you hear the snare and handclap together.

The Yamaha PMC-1 system is similar in that the 'brain' is just a pad-to-MIDI converter (PMC) specifically designed to access the sounds of Yamaha RX series drum machines and FM synth sounds; but it also incorporates more sophisticated editing facilities, rather like the Simmons MTM. *(See Fig. 26)*

The multiple 'daisy-chaining' of MIDI modules, or 'slaves,' from a single controller raises two other aspects of MIDI. With each succeeding slave connected via MIDI

THRU there is a slight time delay. It's therefore advisable with more complex set-ups to use a MIDI THRU box, which only introduces a minimal single delay, common to all units. *(See Fig. 27)*

Note that these slave units will have to operate in MIDI Mode 3 (Omni Off, Poly) if you wish to access them separately. Omni *off* ensures that the units respond to the particular MIDI *channel* they're switched to, rather than to any channel. With Mode 1 (Omni On, Poly), channel information is ignored (see p. 42 for more about MIDI).

You can use your *acoustic* drums to trigger MIDI electronics by miking up the kit and feeding the microphone lines into a trigger-to-MIDI converter. So you can beef up your acoustic sounds with drum machine sounds, Simmons sounds, and so on. *(See Fig. 28)*

Fig. 25

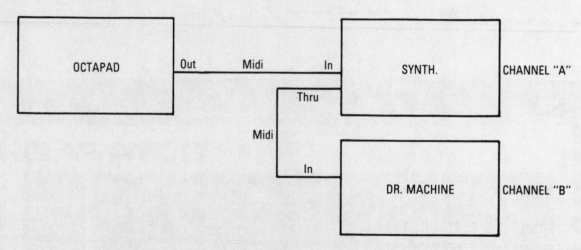

Fig. 26

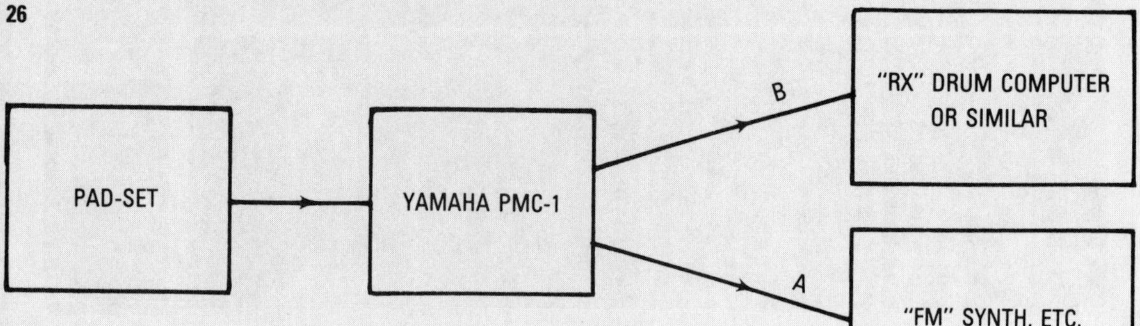

Fig. 27

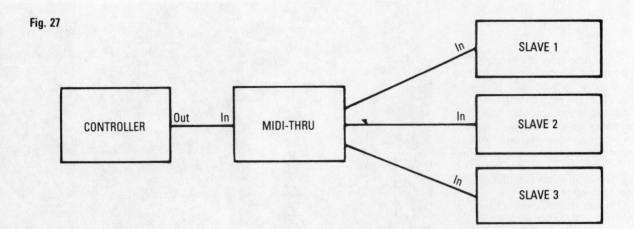

Fig. 28

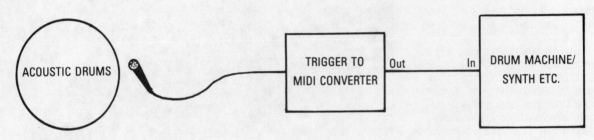

Fig. 29

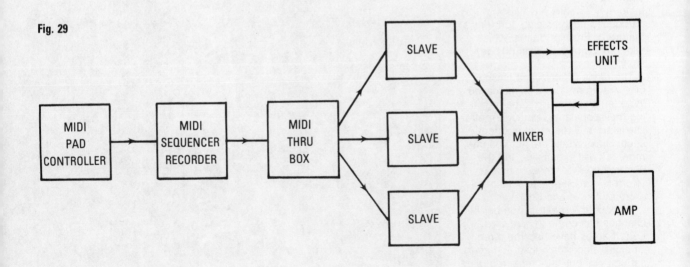

As mentioned earlier, a MIDI *sequencer* can be included in the drum machine or electronic drum set-up. You can have the drum machine control the whole system or, by using pads, you can play in *real time* (see p.110) into the sequencer and digitally record the performance for playback. This allows you to edit or time correct your playing.

Finally, with all the set-ups outlined, it's possible to include effects units. Incorporating, say, a reverb unit and small mixing desk will enable you to add varying amounts of reverb to the snare drum, tom-toms, and so on, and this can greatly enhance live or recorded performance.
(See Fig. 29)

ACOUSTIC DRUMS, CYMBALS AND HARDWARE

The mushrooming of electronic percussion has necessarily affected developments in acoustic drums. The variety in electronic sounds is reflected in the expanded size ranges of acoustic drums; the extra depth and penetration of electronic is reflected in the popularity of 'power' sizes — drums which are deeper in relation to their diameter than normal.

Cymbals manufacturers have also been kept on their toes. In the continuing search for harder, cleaner, louder and more controlled-sounding rides and crashes, there is now an amazing variety of types and sizes on the market, with innovations in finishes from 'Rude' to 'Brilliant,' and even including colors.

Notwithstanding the progress of electronics, acoustic drums are still more popular and continue to develop in fashion and style. Yamaha have been very successful with their relatively lightweight shells using a thin ply of dense hardwood polished on the inside and heavily lacquered on the outside, like a grand piano. This trend has been taken up by other major manufacturers. Yamaha have also reintroduced flush-bracing, formerly a feature of Premier drums, which takes much of the strain off the shell.

The range of sizes and finishes of snare drums has also increased. Wooden shells seem to be regaining their popularity, although metal shells are still the most frequently seen. Brass shells are not uncommon, but are expensive, and the ultimate goal, for those who can afford it, is a one-piece solid maple drum by Noble and Cooley.

Perhaps the greatest number of changes has come in *hardware*. Cage frames have become a regular sight, since they adapt to larger set-ups without the problem of a forest of tripods cluttering up the kit. Another popular innovation is the 'Rims'-type tom-tom mounting. The idea here is for the toms to be supported by a metal collar rather than clamped by a conventional holder. This reduces strain and acoustic deadening. The popularity of double bass drum pedals partly reflects the programming of 'impossible' drum machine beats.

Van Halen stage set-up

Along with double bass drum pedals, remote hi-hats are also becoming popular. These help the drummer to get around the kit more easily and economically and imply a more open-armed approach to playing, an eminently sensible direction developed by American drummer Gary Chester.

FIVE-STRING BASS

Background
The five-string bass has appeared as a direct result of hi-tech synth bass lines. Until a few years ago, most professional bassists were content to play the conventional four-string — perhaps with a fret-less neck, on-board active tone circuitry, and maybe some outboard phase or chorus effects — and were only required to play down to a low E. With the advent of synthesizers, however, keyboard players such as Stevie Wonder, Bernie Worrell, Jan Hammer and Herbie Hancock found it easy to record

Fig. 30

4-String Bass

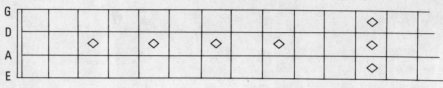

Bottom Ranges Compared

Fig. 31

Keyboard

Fig. 32

5-String Bass

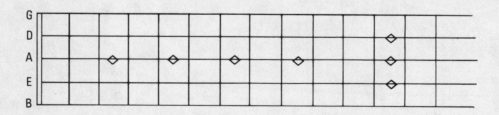

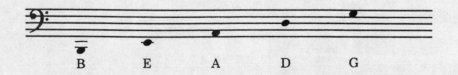

Henry with a 5-string bass

Five-string basses to watch for include the Westone Panterra, Yamaha BB5000, the Status, the Ken Smith, and the Wal.

bass lines that covered a much lower range — for example, E♭ to low C. Given the instant popularity of such a sound, it was time for bass players to get a little nervous!

Synth bass lines quickly became standard on most dance-oriented tracks. Soon, bass players found themselves trying to compete by tuning down the E string. But these efforts only met with string rattle, inconsistent tone and difficult re-tuning. Bass guitars with extra strings had been around since the '60s, but usually with *top* strings tuned to a high C, or in the cases of the Fender VI, two extra strings tuned to B and E. It was now obvious that a *low* fifth string was urgently needed. Hence the arrival of the five-string bass with a low B.

Problems and Solutions

Manufacturers were faced with two initial problems: how to create a string that would reproduce low notes reliably, yet was neither slacker nor harder to play than the other four strings; and how to build an instrument with neck, bridge and pickups to accomodate it.

In America, a company called Ken Smith Guitars began to make high quality five-strings, and in Britain, Electric Wood built a five-string Wal bass while working hand in hand with string manufacturers RotoSound to create the industry standard. Other companies tried fitting five strings onto their four-string models. But the strings were too close together, and players used to wider string spacing found them difficult to play.

Wal opted for normal string spacing on a wider neck, a two octave range, adjustable bridge piece, and parameteric eq with active pickups to home in on those low frequencies.

RotoSound, meanwhile, developed a string made of steel for

brightness and nickel for longevity, which consisted of a central core with seven strands wrapped around it to allow for more flexibility. Two types of finish were provided: regular, with the feel of a roundwound string; and linear, which has the feeling of a flatwound. The playing tension is equal to the other four strings, with an optimum gauge of between 0.135" and 0.140". This string would be combined with a normal light gauge bass set (0.040" — 0.095"), or a standard gauge set (0.105" — 0.128").

Playability

So what is it like to play? Well, when you switch to 'automatic pilot,' it's very easy to think of the bottom string as your reference point. You might finger what you think is a G, and out pops a loud, confident D below it! So there is a necessary adjustment period for altering eye-to-hand coordination.

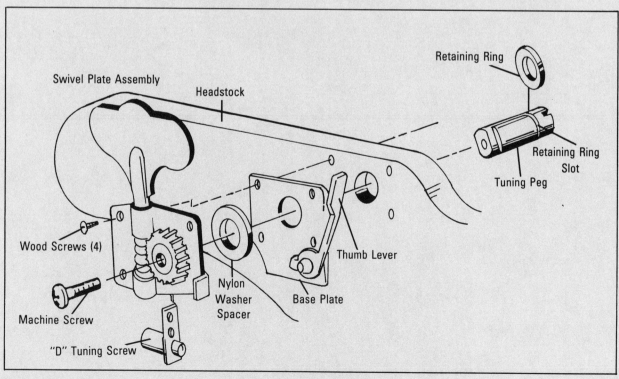

Fig. 33

But soon you're able to perform using all the modern bass techniques.

Like all new toys, there is a temptation to overdo it, leaping from the high registers to speaker-shaking lows. But if you listen to the work of five-string players like Nathan East (George Benson, Kenny Loggins, Phil Collins et al), you'll soon pick up ideas on the economical and *effective* use of the low B.

Producers gave the five-string an immediate and enthusiastic welcome because at last there was a bass that could match the range of synthesizers without losing its own distinctive sound and feel. By now the five-string has become a common sight in the studio in almost all styles of rock.

Check out the playing of John Pattituci (Chick Corea); Jimmy Johnson (Allan Holdsworth's IOU Band); Anthony Jackson (Chaka Khan); and Pino Palladino (Paul Young, Go West).

The Hipshot D-Tuner

Another solution to the problem of playing low notes, which deserves a mention, is the Hipshot D-Tuner. You simply attach this device to the E tuning peg of your four-string bass and by flicking a lever, the string instantly tunes down to a D or C depending on how it's set up. Of course you're faced with having to re-adjust your fingering on the E string every time you change tuning, and there are also problems with intonation due to the change in string tension. But it's cheap and easy to fit to any four-string model. Poll-winning bassist Billy Sheehan (David Lee Roth Band) often uses the Hipshot to help achieve an overall tuning of D, G, D, G. This he finds useful when playing those manic fretboard tapping duets with guitarist Steve Vai!

Finally, there is an instrument called the Overwater C Bass, built by Chris May in 1985. It features an extra long scale length of 36 inches, with the tuning set from low to high at C, F, B♭ and E♭. This is simply a transposition down from the regular E, A, D, G bass tuning. To achieve this, the neck is set further into the body, and the bridge is pushed further back, so that most of the extra length is part of the body.

Overwater C Bass

Overwater 5-string

3 Programming

Stanley Clarke

Introduction

The programming of sounds, rhythms and sequences is a vital part of modern musicianship. It goes without saying that the skills involved in programming are every bit as 'legitimate' as conventional instrumental playing techniques (for keyboard techniques see p.16 ; for updates on guitar, bass and drumming techniques, refer to table of contents; for basic guitar, bass and drumming techniques, see companion volume *ROCK-SCHOOL 1 — Guitar, Bass, Drums*). Before you can get into programming proper, however, you have to understand a little about what synthesis is and how synthesizers work.

What is Synthesis?

Synthesis is the combining of several component parts or elements into one unified 'whole.' In physics, synthesizing certain colors produces white light. In philosophy, it is the gathering together of lots of pieces of information, and observations, into one cohesive point of view. You get the picture.

And it's the same in musical terms: to synthesize a sound you are combining all the elements that, together, produce sound: pitch, loudness, and timbre. (For more on the basics of sound, see p.12).

Fortunately, you need to know surprisingly little about the physics of sound in order to understand, at least in theory, how to program a synthesizer — be it analog, digital, steam powered, thought-controlled, you name it.

But before we get down to business what *is* the difference between an analog and a digital synth?

Analog synthesizers

An analog synthesizer is one whose sounds are produced and manipulated by a continuously variable electric current. The basic concept of an analog synth is that you start off by electronically generating a waveform, and then you knock it into shape by pulling and pushing it and filtering out all the unwanted bits. This is called *subtractive* synthesis.

Until recently almost all production models were analog, from the MiniMoog, Roland SH-1, Korg MS-10, to the Prophet-5, Oberheim OB-8, Yamaha CS-80, to the Roland Juno-60, and the Korg Poly 800.

Digital synthesizer

A digital synthesizer is one whose sounds are manipulated by a series of numbers — just two in fact: 0s and 1s, repeated over and over. Accordingly, *all* its commands can be given and understood by microprocessors.

The fundamental difference between an analog and a digital synth is that instead of applying all manner of electronic circuitry to a basic waveshape in order to remove unwanted portions, a digital synth simply multiplies sine waves together. And by the cunning means of varying the waves' frequency and/or loudness, you can create an enormously wide range of complex tone colors. This is called *additive* synthesis.

Inside an analog synthesizer

The three main groups of controls of an analog synth govern the three primary elements of sounds: pitch, loudness, and timbre.

VCO (Voltage Controlled Oscillator), controlling pitch, and basic tone.

VCA (Voltage Controlled Amplifier), controlling loudness.

VCF (Voltage Controlled Filter), controlling timbre or tone.

There are two equally important additional groups:

Envelope Generator, which is used to shape a sound or part of a sound.

LFO (Low Frequency Oscillator), which is used for modulation.

VCO

The oscillator section is the heart of a synthesizer. This is where the basic sounds come from. Invariably you will be offered a choice of basic waveforms, amongst which will be:

Sine: which contains no harmonics, and is a pure tone, good for adding in with other waveforms, or for whistles, and sundry 'electronic' noises;

Sawtooth: which is made up entirely of harmonics, is rich and bright, and is good for strings and brass sounds;

Pulse: which is a variable odd-harmonic waveform whose harmonics can be progressively filtered out. How many harmonics remain is down to the pulse width control. At 50% the wave will contain *all* the odd harmonics, and is then called a square wave. 'Narrow' pulse waves produce thin, nasal tones, good for spiky sounds like a clarinet, or guitar.

Square: see pulse. They sound hollow, and are good for clarinets and other woody tones.

Triangle: contains only the odd harmonics, but at a lower level than square wave, and so duller.

ANALOG SYNTHS

Advantages: Generally easier to understand. Through being less stable, can sound more human.

Disadvantages: Less stable — as far as tuning is concerned — more expensive to produce — lots of knobs and switches — less precise — 'Yesterday's technology.'

Remember: An instrument that sports DCOs (digitally controlled oscillators) is not necessarily a digital synth. Invariably it is simply that the instrument's oscillators are controlled *digitally* for greater tuning stability.

DIGITAL SYNTHS

Advantages: Wider range of sounds available through increased precision — stability — 'Today's/tomorrow's technology'

Disadvantages: Initially more complex to program.

Good for recorders and other woodwinds.

All older, monophonic synths offered wide control over pitch on their oscillator sections. This was normally represented in octave jumps as 8', 16', 4', like organ stops (these figures being a hang-over from the days when the physical length of organ pipes determined the pitch of the notes they produced). You could also expect to find a fine tuning control between two or more oscillators, which could then produce a form of phasing to thicken up the sound.

On more recent polyphonic synths you may find these controls have been streamlined, offering only fine tuning between two or more oscillators, and a simple 'octave' switch for the sound as a whole.

Sync

This feature is found only on instruments with two or more oscillators per voice. What it does is force the oscillators to play in tune with each other even if you have 'detuned' them. This can produce a variety of effects, from an increase in the harmonic content of a sound to increased punchiness.

LFO/ENV Switch

This feature relates to control over the width of a pulse wave. Under 'normal' circumstances its width can be set manually, with a slider, but an LFO/ENV switch indicates you have the option of controlling the width from the LFO or from an envelope generator, which can introduce more life or movement into a sound.

Sub oscillator

This is easy. A sub oscillator is a simple tool to fatten up a sound. It simply joins forces with the other oscillator(s) at a specified pitch (normally one or two octaves) below. Usually a sub oscillator is preset as a square wave.

Noise

Noise is found in or around the oscillator panel as a separate sound generator. It produces a whole series of random frequencies that have, as such, no musical content. Noise just hisses. White noise contains all frequencies and is brighter than pink noise, which concentrates on lower frequencies. Apart from noise's obvious application, for producing steam, wind, and thunder effects, it can be added into a sound to simulate breathiness, or a hint of 'electronic' percussion.

Ring modulator

This isn't actually part of an oscillator section but its job concerns the oscillators. It accepts the signal from two oscillators and churns out both the sum of their frequencies and the difference between their frequencies. The result is all sorts of wonderful overtones and harmonics — lots of them — and is ideal for creating gongs and bells and such.

Cross modulation

Again this feature is not strictly part of the oscillator 'panel' but, as does a ring modulator, it concerns one oscillator's effect upon another, in this instance the use of one oscillator to modulate the other. Unlike an LFO, which modulates oscillators with very low frequencies — too low to actually hear, in order to produce vibratos, etc. —

modulating one regular audio oscillator with the output from another, produces all manner of weird and wonderful overtones and harmonics, similar (in effect) to those produced by using a ring modulator.

VCA

This is not nearly as complex to understand as the VCO. A VCA governs loudness, and is really just a glorified volume control. However, certain parameters can be routed to the VCA, such as the LFO or envelope generator, which in turn then control or shape the volume of a sound. Most VCA panels consist of a single slider, but sometimes you'll have some options like Hold, Gate, or Env, as well. Selecting Hold will make a sound play continuously, even after you lift your fingers off the keys. Gate clips off the note(s) as soon as you stop playing, and selecting Env will put the shape of the note under the control of the envelope generator.

VCF

A filter, as its name implies, filters out certain aspects of a sound's make-up (harmonics) and so acts as a form of tone control. There are several different types of filters, and these can work in conjunction with several other sections of a synthesizer such as the LFO, and the envelope generator.

There are four basic modes of filtering: Low pass, high pass, band pass, and notch. Of these, the low pass is the one most commonly found on synthesizers, and, not coincidentally, the most useful.

You recall that all waveforms (except sine waves) contain harmonics (see p. 13). A low pass filter filters out high harmonics and lets the low harmonics *pass* through. Precisely which harmonics are allowed to pass depends upon a parameter called the Cut-off Frequency control, which sets the point at which filtering starts or stops, in other words where it *cuts off.*

The point at which a filter *cuts off* is, incredibly enough, called the cut-off point. Frequencies at this level can be boosted by a parameter called Resonance, sometimes referred to as Q. Boosting these frequencies causes a sound to burble, resonate, and ring out. If these frequencies are boosted to their

ADDITIONAL VCO FEATURES:
Sync — LFO/ENV Switch — Sub Oscillator — Noise — Ring Modulator — Cross Modulation

maximum amount, the sound becomes pure sine wave feedback. You can then 'play' the filter, which can be surprisingly useful for re-creating the pure sound of a flute.

2-pole/4-pole: This rating tells you how quickly a filter is dispatching 'unwanted' harmonics. A 2-pole filter reduces the volume of 'unwanted' harmonics by 12db per octave and a 4-pole by 24db per octave. In other words, a 2-pole filter doesn't cut-off the harmonics as sharply as a 4-pole. Many synths offer the option of 2-pole/4-pole filtering.

High pass filter: This works similarly to the low pass except that it is low frequencies that can be progressively filtered out. Normally instruments that include a high pass filter simply offer slider control over the cut-off point and no resonance feature.

Band pass filter: This allows only a certain *band* of frequencies to pass through, filtering out all others above and below the selected frequency.

Notch filter: This allows all except a small band of frequencies to pass. It is, in effect, the opposite type to the above.

If you just filter out certain harmonics from a sound, using any of the above types of filters, you may find the sounds still a little lifeless. What breathes life into a sound is movement, tonal changes that occur throughout the note's cycle. To do this you can route the filter through an envelope generator, or through an LFO (see below).

Many synths offer two envelope generators, one to sculpt the filter and one for the overall loudness of the sound. Being able to shape the filtering independently of the VCA envelope generators vastly increases the range of sounds you can program.

Tracking: This feature allows the pitch of your note to variably control the cut-off point of the filter. It's most useful for 'toning down' screechy high frequencies when you're playing in the upper registers, or for providing a bit of 'bite' on low notes.

Envelope generator

The envelope generator is like a template; it's job is to shape, individually or collectively, all the three main elements of sound — pitch, loudness, and timbre — though in practice only really the latter two. Ideally you will want two separate envelope generators, one to govern loudness (VCA) and one to govern timbre (VCF). Not all synths have such scope though, and you will have to make do with one. A single envelope generator is a limiting factor.

The most common form of envelope generator offers control over four stages of a sound's passage through time: its Attack, Decay, Sustain, and Release.

Attack: controls the front end of a note — how quickly it reaches its peak level (i.e., full volume). Percussive and plucked instruments have a sharp attack, wind instruments or 'slow strings' tend to creep in, comparatively slowly.

Decay: once a sound reaches its peak level it has a choice: either stay at its peak until you stop playing, or gradually settle down to a more comfortable sustain level. How quickly the peak changes into sustain is governed by the decay control.

Sustain: is the level a sound will remain at, until you stop playing.

Release: once you do stop playing, this governs how long the

sound takes to die away, and return to its starting point.

Envelope depth or amount: This governs the overall strength of the ADSR parameters.

LFO

The Low Frequency Oscillator has similarities with regular audio oscillators in that it generates frequencies, and indeed allows you to choose from a number of waveforms, such as sine, square, etc. However, the frequencies generated by the LFO are extremely low — too low to hear — and its job is to modulate (promote continuous changes in) other sections of the synthesizer. Most commonly the LFO is used to create vibratos, tremolo, or trills. Precisely what it does depends upon two things: which waveform it uses, and where it is being directed.

Typical LFO parameters are: Waveform, Rate, Depth, and Delay.

Programming

Programming is a skill, not an art. There is no real mystery about it. The mistake most people make when first confronted by a sea of synth controls is trying to run before they can walk. Rather than lunge at various controls in the hope that, somehow, this great sound will just appear, start by limiting yourself to the simple controls, like the oscillator waveform selector or the VCR cut-off freq control at first. Try to resist the temptation of investigating another batch of controls until you fully understand the ones you're working on.

The oscillator is the heart of your instrument. Waveforms or pitches chosen here decide the basic character of your sound. Some instruments offer just one oscillator per note, others two, others three. As a rule, the more oscillators per note you have the bigger the sound of the instrument, since you can detune the oscillators or set them to play in fourths or fifths.

For Vibrato — a smooth continuous variation in pitch — use a sine wave and apply the LFO to the VCO.

For Trills — a clear-cut, repeated alternation between two notes — use a square wave, and apply the LFO to the VCO.

For Tremolo — a smooth continuous change in volume — use a sine wave and apply the LFO to the VCA.

Wah Wah — a smooth continuous change in tone — use a sine wave and apply the LFO to the filter.

Hints

If you are looking for a specific type of sound, try to analyze some of its characteristics before you start. Is it thick or thin? What type of envelope does it have — fast attack, plucked, smooth, wah wah? The clearer picture you have in your mind before you start, the easier your programming will be.

Here are some starting points for producing specific types of sound:

Voices

WAVEFORM: Pulse — 25%
CUT-OFF FREQ: 60%
RESONANCE: high
VCA ENVELOPE: Slow attack, full sustain, medium/long release.

Brass

WAVEFORM: Sawtooth
CUT-OFF: Off
RESONANCE: Off
FILTER ENVELOPE: Slow attack, sustain 80%
VCA ENVELOPE: Full attack, full sustain.

Clavi

WAVEFORM: Pulse 25%
CUT-OFF FREQ: Full
RESONANCE: Off
VCA ENVELOPE: Full attack, 66% decay, no sustain, no release.

Strings

WAVEFORM: Sawtooth
CUT-OFF FREQ: Full
RESONANCE: Off
FILTER ENVELOPE: very slow attack
VCA ENVELOPE: slow attack, medium release.

Flute

WAVEFORM: Triangle
CUT-OFF FREQ: 25%
RESONANCE: Off
VCA ENVELOPE: medium/fast attack, 50% decay/sustain, short release, plus 'noise' to add breathiness.

Programming a digital synth

By and large, all analog synthesizers have the same parameter groups, the same building blocks for creating sounds. All have oscillators and filters and envelope generators, and in spite of manufacturers' attempts to confuse us by naming some parameters in an alarming variety of ways, we all know (roughly) where we are.

Although the same cannot be said for digital synths, the basic principle of digital synthesis is fairly clear-cut: it is the combination of one waveform with another in order to produce a 'new' sound. A simple example of this is a drawbar organ, where each drawbar corresponds to a different harmonic based on the pitch of the note you play. A wide range of sounds can then be created simply by adding different harmonics and varying their volume levels.

It sounds easy. On an organ it is. But the problem with digital synthesis is that it's not easy (at least it isn't at first) to predict the result of mass addition of sine waves, along with their various envelopes, volumes, and frequencies. Things get more complex still when instead of just combining two waveforms, one waveform is used to

control another, as in FM synthesis popularized by Yamaha. Accordingly, manufacturers are forever looking at ways they can make their digital synths function in as similar a fashion as possible to analog ones.

Fortunately, they don't always have to try too hard. Analog and digital synths do, quite naturally, share several programming parameters — most noticeably the LFO, but also features such as portamento, and, to some extent, envelope generators.

As yet there is no standardization of digital synths. Everybody seems to approach the subject in their own way.

Yamaha FM

Books continue to be written on Digital FM synthesis. There's no way a couple of lines here is going to make life any easier! The principle of FM is relatively straightforward: it uses a number of semi-complete little synthesizers called *Operators*, each blessed with a digital oscillator, a digital amplifier, and a digital envelope generator. On their own the operators simply generate sine waves and accordingly don't sound very interesting. But there are several operators (six on a DX7), and by modulating one with the output from another, and varying the loudness and shape of each, you can produce highly complex sounds. An operator that is used to modulate another is called a *Modulator*, and an operator that is being modulated (or not, as the case may be) is called a *Carrier*. You can combine the operators in a variety of ways by selecting Al-

EDITING OR STARTING FROM SCRATCH?

Undoubtedly, editing a previously stored sound is easier than starting with a clean slate. Flipping through the presets on your synth to find the sound most similar to what you want isn't cheating. It's common sense.

Manufacturer	System	Instruments
Yamaha (FM)	Digital FM Synthesis	DX7, DX9, DX5, DX1, DX27, DX100, DX711, TX816, TX7, TX216 TX216, FB-01, CX5M, TX81Z.
Casio (PD)	Phase Distortion	CZ-101, CZ-1000, CZ-3000, CZ-5000, CZ-230S.
Roland (LAS)	Linear Arithmetic	D-50.
Sequential (VS)	Vector Synthesis	Prophet VS.
Elka	No name	EK-44, EK-44M.
Kawai (DWM)	Digital Wave Memory	K-3, K-3M, K-5, K-5M.
Korg	No name	DS-8.

gorithms — in effect little maps that tell you how the operators are being linked.

FM synths, though rarely well-understood, have been incredibly popular due to the stunning quality of their final sounds. (For more on FM programming, see below).

Elka
A system that bears a striking resemblance to FM.

Kawai DWM
A neat system of digital wave-forms that are then controlled by analog editing parameters. Not only do you have 32 preset waveforms to choose from but you can create your own using the first 128 har-

monics — in other words, true additive synthesis.

Sequential VS
Each voice of Sequential's VS synth can make use of four digital oscillators. Each of the oscillators can either select one of the 128 preset waveforms, or one of a further 32 waveforms that you yourself can create. This you do by adding together some of the presets in an easy, fun, but not terribly precise manner using an XY joystick, which controls their relative balance. Thereafter, you are in analog-type territory, with filters and envelope generators and such. The Prophet VS is rightly renowned for its wide range of high quality, very original sounds.

Casio PD
I don't think anyone truly understands Casio's Phase Distortion method, but this hasn't stopped the company from having tremendous success with a number of PD instruments, for the same reason as Yamaha's FM: they just sound good! Phase Distortion involves distorting the phase angle of a sine wave, through a period of time as set by the envelope of a form of digital filter. Make sense? Well, I said no one really knows what's going on! However, PD synths generally contain a mine of plucky, attacky, useful sounds which you can edit (mainly without a clue what you're doing) and have fun with.

Roland LAS
At the time of this writing there is only one LAS Synthesiser: the D-50. The basic concept is the mixing of two types of waveforms — one a PCM sample of 'real' instruments/sounds, and the other a digitally created waveform. You have a large number of both to choose from and you can combine any of them. Although all the editing parameters are digital, they conform to an analog style and so the instrument is very friendly to use. On this early showing LAS is very promising indeed, and capable of producing highly complex sounds with the least amount of headache.

FM EDITING MADE EASY:

FM is not nearly as simple as the following suggests, but in most — if not all — instances, these procedures will produce the desired effect.

Volume and brightness: increasing the output level of *carriers* will increase your volume level; upping the output level of *modulators* will increase brightness. So, work out which algorithm constitutes your sound and increase the output of each modulator or carrier in turn, until you arrive at the desired volume and brightness.

Attack: change the R1 value for each *operator's* EG in turn until you find the one dealing with attack.

Release: to alter release times, change the R4 value for each operator's EG in turn until the desired effect has taken place.

Vibrato: to get rid of vibrato, reduce *LFO AMD* to 0.

De-tune/chorus: for these effects, adjust the *frequency fine* parameter of the relevant operator.

SAMPLING

Sampling is one of the most challenging methods of sound creation open to today's musician. It can also be one of the most frustrating. And because of the element of frustration, sampling has tended to become something of a sterile occupation; a matter of simply buying, or worse — stealing — sounds already sampled on disc as opposed to recording, editing, and manipulating your own.

Today, sampling may seem a far cry from experiments undertaken at RDTF in France during the 1940s and '50s, when men like Pierre Scheaffer flew around the countryside recording anything that made a noise, then cut up the tapes and pasted them back together in a different context. But in fact although the medium has changed — thanks to the microchip — the problems and pleasures remain remarkably similar. The difference is that while Scheaffer's goal was to produce new, previously unheard-of sounds from an amalgam of natural, everyday noises, we merely seem to want access to natural-sounding sounds that we can't program on a synthesizer, i.e., acoustic instruments or unadulterated sound effects.

Whether this indicates how lazy we have become, or simply that our needs and aspirations have changed, is for you to decide. Either way, the sampling instrument has become part of our lives, and has the honor of being, at the same time, the most complex and the easiest type of instrument to use.

How easy? Very. All current samplers use discs on which the sounds are stored. You buy a sampler, you switch it on, you insert a disc, you play whatever sound is on the disc. The sound could be a full symphony orchestra, a grand piano, a choir of Tibetan monks, a recording of bird noises . . . In effect, these discs are no more mysterious than a bunch of presets

on a regular polyphonic synth—except that they are stored externally.

Most samplers are sold complete with a selection of 'sounds' plus the option of buying more sounds from the manufacturers' own sound library. There is no shame using a sampler solely as a preset, *replay* machine. In fact, 90% of users do just that!

This is all well and good — except in the eyes of the Musicians Union, who, with some justification, see samplers as having a disastrous effect upon the livelihoods of brass, wind and string players. But the brass, wind and string players' trump card is that playing, say, a sax solo on a keyboard sampler, is no easy matter. OK, so the sound may physically be that of a saxophone, but the basic sound of an instrument is by no means the whole story.

Firstly, the physical design of a sax governs both what you play and variations in tonality. Certain notes may sound weak and so are avoided. Certain runs or licks may be easy on a sax, and so are played often. The same run or lick may be a nightmare to play on a keyboard. A mere sample of a sax stored on a disc cannot take this unique tonality into consideration.

Samplers don't find it easy to 'tongue,' or 'overblow' or perform any of the other tricks of the trade (though this problem can be solved on more sophisticated samplers using velocity switching — assigning two different sounds to each note; one to sound when you strike the key hard, the other when playing softly). Nor do most samplers cater for the minute but important changes in tone throughout a saxophone's range.

What is stored on your sax disc will be the sound of a saxophone sampled at a number of different pitches (seldom, if ever, every single note in its range), and what the sampler will do is 'fill in' the spaces by speeding up or slowing down those samples so that you can play all the notes of the scale on your keyboard.

Herein lies another problem — one that again varies from sampler to sampler, or disc to disc. The authenticity of a 'real-instrument' sample depends upon how many times the instrument in question has been sampled throughout its natural range. If, say, you merely have one sample of a sax playing middle C, then by the time you play much more than one octave above or below middle C, I guarantee it will sound pretty daft. Either it'll squawk at you like some sort of cheap toy, or it'll sound lugubriously drunk. This is because one basic sound is simply being sped up or slowed down to produce all the different pitches, and after only a small amount of fluctuation from its original pitch, it just sounds absurd.

This syndrome, believe it or not, is called *munchkinization*. And you avoid it by multi-sampling, i.e., sampling a sound several times at several different pitches. Or rather, hopefully, someone else has already done this for you on your factory/library disc.

User Sampling

Most of us, however content we are with using previously sampled sounds, are at least curious about sampling sounds for ourselves. And it doesn't take long to discover that this is rarely a simple operation, unless you're content sampling yourself going 'duh duh duh' and using that to drive the neighbors mad.

To sample successfully, you do need to understand what some of the jargon surrounding sampling really means.

Almost all instruments come supplied with spec. sheets, telling you things like its signal-to-noise ratio, how heavy the instrument is, etc., etc. But on sampler spec. sheets you'll also find things like this:

*Sample Frequency (or Rate):
10kHz – 40kHz
Sample Times: 10 sec – 50 sec*

Sampling is the business of capturing a sound in some storage and retrieval system and then retriggering or 'playing' it back — normally, but not invariably, from a keyboard.

Multi-sampling: 32
Data Format: 12-bit
Bandwidth: 20Hz – 20kHz
Storage: built-in 3.5 inch disc
drive.

If this looks forbidding, don't worry, it's a lot easier to understand than you might think. Let's dispense with the really easy stuff first.

Data Format: You don't need to know precisely what the figure means. It is simply an indication of the sampler's ability to handle data — how much at a time, how fast. In practice, all you need to know is that the bigger the number the better the instrument. 8-bit is okay but limited, 12-bit is good, 16-bit is very good, and 32-bit (should it arrive on regular instruments) will be spectacular.

Storage: This tells what (if any) type of discs are used to store your sounds. Once again, there is no mystique about it, but in general the bigger the disc the more information it can hold, and the more information a disc can hold the better. The 2.8 inch Quick Discs are currently quite common on low-cost instruments, and though they do their job, they can only hold small amounts of information.

Sample Times, Sample Frequency and Bandwidth are all inter-related. They tell you how long your samples can be and how good they'll sound, and there is a trade off between the length of your sample and how good it'll sound.

Sample Time means just that. In our example the instrument can sample sounds up to 50 seconds in duration. Yes, but why the 10

seconds before it? You may not always be given two figures, but if you are it relates to the maximum length of time that you can sample for at the *top quality rate*. Remember the trade-off?

So you can set your machine at a high Sample Rate, say 40kHz, and then have to make do with just 10 seconds of Sample Time. On the other hand, if you must have 40 or 50 seconds available (maybe you want to sample a whole chorus of a song), then you must sacrifice quality. Quality means just that. At a high Sample Rate, what you put in will come back almost identical. At a low rate, it'll come back noisy and rather dull. Think of the trade-off like gasoline consumption in a car. You can either save gas by driving slower or get there faster by using more. What the Sample Rate figure actually tells you is the sampler's ability to 'hear' or accept sound data. If it can work up to 42kHz then it's up to Compact Disc specification, and it doesn't get much better after that. So the higher the number the better quality the sample(r). Bandwidth refers to what you can hear out of the instrument, and the higher number is normally half the Sample Rate. Beyond 20kHz, you are practically in dog-whistle territory!

The Multi-sampling figure tells you how many samples can be held at any one time, and so if necessary spread across the keyboard range to re-create a munchkinization-free sound!

The initial sampling of a sound is seldom difficult. Depending upon the sampler you may have to go through certain procedures like choosing a Sample Rate, specifying a sample length, and checking your

"When we're improvising, I tend to switch on the sampler without necessarily telling Mike (Rutherford) and Phil (Collins) that I'm doing it. And once, I got 17 seconds of what was mainly Mike playing the guitar. I cut up a little slice of that which I thought was interesting. And by combining two notes, one of which was faster than the original and one of which was much slower, I had a song almost written! And that song became 'The Brazilian' on our current LP ('Invisible Touch')."

TONY BANKS

input level (just like on a tape machine), but these become second nature after a very short time. No, it's what you may have to do *afterwards* that's the pain in the neck.

Truncating and Looping

Immediately you have made your sample, you'll want to play it back on the keyboard. You play a note . . . there's a bit of noise and then . . . there it is: duh duh duh. Brilliant. But, ideally, you'd rather not have that bit of noise before duh duh duh begins, so you must 'truncate' the sample, i.e., lop off the said unwanted bit of noise. On most samplers not only can you lop off bits of the beginning, but bits of the end too. Duh duh duh can so become duh duh du, or uh duh du.

Now you may feel it unlikely that you'll ever want duh duh duh duh duh . . . and on and on forever, but when you get to sampling a musical note, I can assure you that looping the sound is precisely the facility you'll be after.

HOW TO GET THE BEST FROM A SAMPLER WITHOUT ACTUALLY HAVING TO SAMPLE!!

As already mentioned, there is no sin in using factory/library discs on a sampler. You will be in good company. However you'll get far more pleasure from 'real instrument' sounds with a little research and practice into the capabilities of and techniques behind the instruments themselves.

Pay attention to the style of playing on the 'real instrument.' Try to use the same voicing. In other words, if you want to recreate the sound of an acoustic guitar strumming the chord of A minor, then work out which actual notes a guitarist would play.

Listen to how brass players phrase. They need to take breaths. On a keyboard, of course, you don't. But to sound authentic, you should take breaks and not fly about all over the keyboard in a never-ending whirr of notes. If you want to create the feel of a brass section, then listen to a brass section and work out each individual part. Then you will learn how that sound is created.

Avoid playing in registers that are out of range on the real instrument.

Tony Banks ▷

SAMPLING AND THE LAW

Sounds: As yet there is no law against sampling Joe Blow's lovingly-created snare drum sound off record and using it yourself. However this *is* stealing, and if for none other than moral reasons, should be avoided.

Disc copying: Again, despite manufacturers' efforts to cover themselves, there is little they can do to stop you copying, from disc to disc, a sound that someone else has purchased. The only factor to bear in mind is that should the majority of people start doing this then no one will bother 'selling' such sounds in the first place.

Looping is exactly what it sounds like, 'joining up' a sound so that it plays continuously. Almost all samplers include this facility and, though some make the feature easier to use than others (sometimes offering an auto-loop function), it is rarely a straightforward operation. Finding the ideal 'loop point,' so that the sound plays smoothly, without any 'click' in the middle, is made simpler when you can see the waveform on screen. Thus it may be worth considering an 'Editor' program, run on a personal computer. Editor programs have been written for most of today's samplers.

Changing the sound of a sample

Most samplers offer a plethora of analog-style editing parameters that can be used to shape or fine tune your sound once sampled. These include LFO's, envelope generators, and filters, exactly like those you find on an analog synthesizer. These parameters can be very useful to disguise sounds that everyone else seems to have, and/or to give you the chance of just being creative!

General hints on sampling

1. In order to save memory, do a little homework on a sound

"I did it on the last album (the "Genesis" LP), by taking something from a classical record. I was originally trying to get a decent string sound but the record I had was so scratched, it sounded terrible. So what I actually got was three notes. By looping that and then playing a chord, I got each group of three notes moving at different speeds and in different keys and it gave a lovely effect. But it was by pure chance."
TONY BANKS

before sampling it. If you can roughly work out a sound's bandwidth then you can

Akai S900

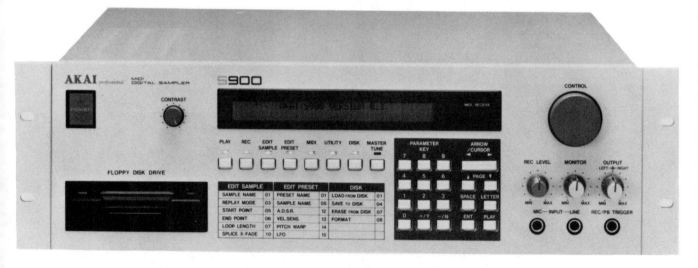

Instead of stealing other people's sounds, why not steal your own? If you've got sounds you like on a non-touch sensitive synth, you can sample them and use the *expression* controls available on the sampler to give more range to the sound, and then, via MIDI, play it using a touch sensitive keyboard.

CREATIVE SAMPLING SUMMARIZED:

You can stack or layer two or more different sounds on top of one another — a sharp, percussive noise over an acoustic guitar, for example. If your sampler can't do this, MIDI it up to a synth and use the percussive sound in your sampler simply as the attack portion of your overall sound. Remember that samplers with a layering capability can layer as many sounds at once as they are able to store. The Akai S-900, for example, stores 32 samples — and you can play all 32 at once by assigning them to one key.

If you don't want to get into extremes, you can instead create an easy-to-play brass section by assigning three differently pitched brass samples to one key.

Use the sampler as a compact alternative to MIDI. By combining different sounds — with or without effects already added — you can dispense with having to carry around loads of different synths and MIDI leads to get the sounds you want live.

If you have a synth without a split keyboard, sample the different sounds you wish to split and assign them to different parts of your sampler's keyboard.

Repair timing and tuning mistakes made during recording by sampling the offending part and then dropping it in manually in the correct time, or at the correct pitch by using the pitch wheel.

choose a sample rate to suit. There's no point, for example, in selecting a high sample rate for a sound with few, or no, high harmonics.

2. If your sound plays back brighter than the original, your sample rate has been set too high; duller than the original, too low.

3. As with tape recording, make sure you sample at the optimum level to reduce noise.

4. Don't run before you can walk. If you are new to sampling, start by recording short, percussive, effects-type sounds. To re-create the exact sound and feel of 'real instruments' is not easy.

PLAYING BASS SYNTH

The bass guitar is still in the main a *supportive* instrument whose function is to supply the root of the chord and the bottom end of the band's sound. But at the same time, it has evolved into a *lead* instrument through the pursuit of fresh harmonic and melodic ideas by players like Jack Bruce, John

Entwistle, Billy Sheehan, Stanley Clarke, Jeff Berlin and many others. Better amps, speakers and effects have also helped to enhance the bass sound. But most recently, the emergence of dedicated bass guitar synthesizer systems and guitar-to-MIDI interfaces (see p. 49) has put the bassist in touch with an almost limitless catalogue of new sounds. Even in its traditional role, the bass will never sound quite the same again.

Problems

It may seem rather negative to begin this section with the heading 'problems.' But, as with dedicated *guitar* synthesizer controllers, you need to play a bass synth with a certain amount of care. Earlier in this book I looked at the Roland GR 77B system (p. 58), which I've used in the studio, in the *ROCK-SCHOOL* TV shows, and on the road. Let me share with you some of the things I've learned about getting the best from this instrument.

Most playing problems really occur when the bassist defeats the envelope of the patch he or she is

playing. The first rule of synthesis is (or should be) to play the patch, that is, play *inside* the sound you are using and imagine how that instrument would perform. A flute-like sound, for example, will be more effective if the player attempts to 'breathe' and phrase like a real flautist. So should synth players imitate other instruments? Not necessarily. But the important fact about sounds is that they do fall into general categories. As well as trying to imitate old sounds, you can and should create new ones. You will certainly have to learn something about programming, and MIDI. But what's a few months' work getting to grips with new technology in comparison to the years it takes to master the bass guitar? (For more on programming, see p. 98.)

As with guitar synths (see p. 50), you need to make sure that your picking is clean and that all unwanted notes are lightly dampened. When a string is plucked it creates sympathetic resonances from the other strings, and these will come out at the same volume as the note you've plucked. The synth only wants to read the main note, so you're going to have to

Step into another instrumentalist's shoes and open up some new frontiers!

modify your technique, and you can adjust the touch sensitivity of the synth to help you do this. Remember, you are not playing a bass guitar; you're playing a synthesizer!

Delay

All pitch-to-voltage guitar synth systems have a delay of some kind. The GR 77B's delay is fortunately only really noticeable on the bottom strings. If you have a part that you normally play on the bottom strings and the delay factor is inhibiting you, you can play the same part an octave higher on the neck, and transpose the synth patch down an octave.

Also, try practicing to drum machine beats, playing synth sounds with a muted bass. After a while you will automatically adjust your timing to play ahead of the beat so that your synth sounds in time.

In a live situation where your synth and bass sounds are combined, adjusting the two will help balance out any unwanted delay. In the studio, moreover, you can always play the parts into a sequencer and quantize-out the delay. For step-time programming, it's possible to calculate the delay factor on each string in milliseconds. The frequencies in hertz of the open strings, for example, are as follows:

```
OPEN STRINGS   E   41.235 Hz
               A   55.000 Hz
               D   73.416 Hz
               G   97.990 Hz
```

Using the equation $100 \div Hz$ frequency gives you the delay on each open string, thus:

```
OPEN STRINGS   E   0.0243
                   Msecs
               A   0.0182
                   Msecs
               D   0.0136
                   Msecs
               G   0.0102
                   Msecs.
```

The GR 77B will digitally process even those sounds that are normally inaudible on a standard bass guitar. If you don't play a clear pitched note, all you get is a funny noise!

Live Performance

Spend a little time going through the factory presets and experimenting with different combinations. Some interesting effects can be discovered by playing simple bass lines against a rich chordal backdrop (see p.174 for some ideas on chord voicings). Similarly, you can play a bass solo against an organ or Rhodes patch, giving the impression of a sparse keyboard accompaniment. In either case, the backdrop can be brought in and out by using the 'hold' pedal on the synth. Other ideas include:

1. Slow blues licks played in unison with a trombone sound.

2. Using the 'string selection group' to give different sounds to different strings; so, by keeping a normal bass sound for the E and A strings and selecting, say, a trumpet sound for the D and G strings, you can play brass fills over a low funk pattern.

3. Drum sounds accessed via MIDI from a synth module (in my case, the Yamaha FB01), assigned to different notes — the bottom E string becomes a bass drum, the A string a snare, and the G string a ride cymbal!

   The bass guitar synthesizer brings the bassist into the realms of serious experimentation and orchestration — especially with the help of MIDI. Say you have a song you want to arrange. You can lay down brass, strings, keyboard and percussion parts in demo format; then, in the studio, you have the option of using other keyboard sounds or real instruments. By loading parts into a sequencer, furthermore, you can play around with different textures without going down onto tape. With this instrument, the only barriers to your playing are the limits of your imagination.

John Entwistle

Combining variations on pianos, voices and strings seems to work well, as does brass, electric piano and flute; try putting together sounds which complement one another, avoiding similar attack and sustain times.

CREATIVE SEQUENCING

Step Time/Real Time Recording

Most sequencers offer you a choice between Step Time and Real Time recording — terms that refer to the two basic methods of programming your sequencer. To program a sequencer in Real Time is to play into it, like you would into a tape recorder. Your performance is then captured *in real time* even though you can go on to edit, correct timing errors, change keys, etc. In Step time, you program each note and timing value individually — *step by step*.

Which method you choose largely depends upon your grasp of musical notation, since with Step Time recording you must tell the sequencer precisely which note(s) to play, when, and for how long — all in musical terms, rather as one would on manuscript paper. Although much slower, the main advantage of this approach is that you can devise and record with perfect accuracy passages that go far beyond your own manual dexterity on the keyboard.

Step Time

There's no mystery to Step Time recording. It is a simple matter of inputting notes and timing values, one after the other, until your sequence is complete. Note information is normally input from your connected keyboard, and timing values from the sequencer. If you want your sequence simply to be, say, a run of sixteenths, you can normally just set the timing value in advance and then all notes input will automatically play as sixteenths. For more complex passages, however, you will have to assign a note value for each note played which, even though it can get rather fiddly, is not difficult.

Real Time

Although on the face of it Real Time programming is by far the easier method, there are still a number of areas where you can come unstuck. The beauty of Real Time recording is that one's *performance* is captured — little inflections here, different emphases there — and yet once the performance has been captured you can still change tempo, key, or sound setting.

However, no matter how good your sense of rhythm, one of the most important features to pay attention to is the quantize, or auto-correct factor. An ideal quantize setting will allow just the right amount of player personality to come through while keeping the sequence strictly in time.

Quantizing irons out your timing discrepancies, to a greater or lesser extent depending on the quantize factor. Manufacturers use all manner of different words to describe both quantizing (auto-correct, resolution, etc.) and the feature's various levels of operation. But the smaller the fraction (1/64th, 1/96th, etc.), the less the quantize will pull your playing into shape. The fraction corresponds to the smallest note value that the sequencer will accept on playback. So, by setting a quantize factor of 1/16th for a sequence in 4/4 time, no matter how fast you play, the sequence will not play back notes shorter than sixteenths. Similarly, a quantize factor of 1/8th will not play back anything smaller than eighths.

The trick, of course, is deciding which is best for your particular sequence. Although this can be a matter of simple trial and error, as a rule of thumb if you've worked out that the smallest note in your sequence is a quaver (an 1/8th note), then select the next highest quantize factor, i.e., 1/16th. If you select the exact quantize equivalent to your sequence's 'smallest note,' you may find that the result is too metronomic and stiff.

Tips

1. The more preparatory work you do, the easier all sequencing will be. Work out the total number of bars to sequence. Work out how many sections repeat, and use the repeat or copy function on your sequencer. This saves time in recording, and memory.
2. If your sequencer can choose to accept such data as pitch bend, after touch and the like, delete all such information you are not going to need. All these performance parameters gobble up memory at a frightening rate.
3. When recording a short riff or collection of notes you will want to repeat over and over, remember to end your 'take' on the last note at the end of the phrase. This may sound obvious, but it's all too easy to complete a passage by ending on the first note of the next bar — and then you wonder why, when programmed to repeat, it has this wretched glitch in it.
4. When recording a tricky passage, rehearse it first, and, if necessary, slow down the metronome speed until the passage is comfortable to play.
5. Whenever possible, play to a drum machine rather than just the built-in metronome. A drum machine beat is generally a little more inspiring.

ADVANTAGES OF STEP TIME:

1. Accuracy: Provided you know what you want, Step Time recording does away with fiddling about with quantize settings and having to slow down the recording of a passage in order (at least!) to get the notes right.
2. For those with no keyboard skills: you may be a great musician but not a keyboard player. If so, then Step Time recording is the one for you.
3. For learning how to write musical notation: write out your sequence beforehand (if you have the notation skills to write in Step Time in the first place this shouldn't be a problem), with bar numbers, phrasing and repeats, etc. Transfering from real manuscript paper to 'electronic manuscript paper' will then be extremely simple.

Remember, sequencers do not record *sound*, they record *information*.

Synchronization

This is the real nightmare aspect of sequencing. It all sounds so simple in theory. In practice . . .

A A A A R R G G H H !

The basic problem with synchronizing a sequencer to drum machines, or to other sequencers, or to a code from tape, is that ever since the arrival of MIDI, not only are there several ways of doing it but there are a *zillion* 'black boxes' on the market, all of which claim to provide the only foolproof answer to all the questions.

If you are only using a MIDI sequencer and a MIDI drum machine, and all you want is for them to play in time with each other, then all well and good. You're unlikely to run into problems. But maybe you'd like your sequencer to 'chase' your drum machine (if you start at bar 32 on your master device, you want the slave device to follow, and not start again at bar 1), in which case *both devices* must implement MIDI Song Pointers. There again you might want to work with one of the excellent older drum machines, like Roland's TR-808. And then there are time codes, like SMPTE. Mixing and matching can be fun, but stock up on aspirin!

Clock Rates

The reason time-based devices like sequencers and drum machines play so accurately is because they are being driven by a stream of electronic pulses generated by an internal clock. The speed of these pulses is measured in ppqn, or pulses per quarter note. In other words, if a sequencer runs at 24 ppqn, every pulse nudges the sequence forward by 1/24th of a beat (a beat being a crotchet or quarter note). Problems occured frequently before MIDI, because every manufacturer had their own idea about which ppqn number was best for

their instrument. Roland used 24, Korg used 48, Obereim used 96, PPG — 64, etc., etc. This meant that if you connected a 24ppqn Roland device to a 48ppqn Korg device, the Korg would play at twice the speed.

Tape Codes

If you record a stream of trigger pulses onto your multi-track tape, then your drum machine and sequencer can use this 'code' as their timing master. What's the point? Because if the tape is continually giving out timing instructions, then in theory you do not have to record the sequencer and drum machine. You can simply have the sequencer and drum machine playing 'live' in sync with the rest of the recording, thus saving valuable tracks and recording time.

Unfortunately, as with the devices themselves, there are many different types of code, and many coverter boxes to go with them:

FSK (Frequency Shift Keying): Instead of dealing in on/off type pulses, FSK uses a periodic shift between two pitches as its clocking method. In some cases, FSK may be more stable than pulse codes.

SMPTE: This 24-hour time-based code was developed by the Society of Motion Picture and Television Engineers in the '60s to facilitate synchronization of movie soundtracks with the action on film. Although used extensively in professional recording studios, you are unlikely to come across it on the average sequencer or drum machine. SMPTE code doesn't just keep things in time; it keeps track of where you are on tape, since it is based on a 24-hour clock. Positions are measured in hours, minutes, seconds, frames, and bits or subframes.

MTC (MIDI Time Code): This is still hot off the press and, as of this writing, only one instrument

(Sequential's Studio 440) has implemented it. MTC is a protocol for sending SMPTE information over MIDI, and, as such, might do away with the current necessity for special SMPTE/MIDI interfaces.

Sequencing Footnotes

Arpeggiators: These are most commonly seen simply as another feature on a synthesizer. They play — automatically — notes held down on your keyboard, at variable speeds and ranges. Although an arpeggiator is not a sequencer substitute (you cannot 'program' more than a few notes at a time), they can be superb for creating simple sequencer-like effects, where all you need is a simple, constant, repetitive riff.

Noise Gates: Another way to produce sequencer-like effects is to use the 'key input' of a noise gate. By feeding, say, the hi-hat into the key input and patching in your synth, every time the noise gate hears the hi-hat it will allow the signal from your synth to pass through. You, meanwhile, are simply playing along. The result is that the hi-hat pattern triggers your playing. The results, apart from being perfectly in time with the hi-hat, can be marvellously weird and wonderful, with all sorts of cross rhythms and feels.

Sequencers and Bass Lines

Let's look at one area of playing where you can use a sequencer to help you create interesting and unusual effects with your bass lines. The bass guitar is an incredibly expressive instrument possessing almost endless tonal possibilities, most of which are immediately available at your finger tips. Let me remind you of a few:

the clear bell-like ring of a thumb note; the hard aggressive whack of a plucked note; the clicking toppy sound of strumming the strings with your fingernails; muted sounds made by left and right hand damping; the tight hard sound of picking at the bridge; the punchy, more rounded sound caused

ADVANTAGES OF REAL TIME:

1. Immediacy. It's generally quick to operate.
2. To capture a performance, rather than a selection of notes (Step Time can also be programmed with dynamics and staccato/legato phrases, but this takes a care and patience).

MIDI Clock runs at 24ppqn. Accordingly, two MIDI devices will automatically play in time with each other, no matter who made them.

by playing over the pickup; the soft bassy sound made by picking near the neck; swoops, slurs, trills and slides, etc., etc....

In the hothouse of the recording studio, however, these subtle nuances of expression may end up sounding like a bunch of badly

played squeaks and rattles! So when laying down a bass part, producers will often aim for an 'unnatural' evenness of phrasing, tone and attack over the required range of the instrument, perfect intonation, and accurate timing. And that's where a sequencer comes in, with the bass line being loaded

in either from a bass guitar or a synthesizer.

To preserve a live feel, accents or fills may be added by the bass over the top of the sequencer. Or, more interestingly, you can *incorporate* the natural dynamics of your playing into the sequenced line, as in the following example.

Fig. 34

Fig. 35

Record a bass line onto cassette and analyze its component parts. Treat each dynamic as a different synth sound and load that part into a sequencer. Work with the keyboard player in your bank if you don't have access to synth sounds yourself. You will build up a very workable composition, while sparking off more ideas for playing around the sequencer lines with the bass.

Here are four bars of a piece that I played on a *ROCKSCHOOL* TV show: *(See Fig. 34)*

From this complete pattern, the line was broken down into four motifs:

1) The low notes of the pattern are replaced by a Moog-type sound;

2) The inner rhythms are replaced by a muted percussive sound;

3) The bass 'snaps' of the right hand sound good as hard, aggressive brass fills;

4) Finally, the harmonics are replaced by a 'bell' sound.

Once the sequencer has taken over, the bass just adds fills over the backing, playing around a Bm9 chord. *(See Fig. 35)*

Used in this way, a sequencer becomes not just a tool for copying an existing part or reproducing programs that your fingers cannot play: it becomes a creative instrument in its own right.

PLAYING DRUM MACHINES

Step-time, Real-time and Quantizing

The programming of drum machines varies with different models, of course. But there are certain principles which they all share. Basically, drum rhythms or patterns are recorded in 'real' or 'step' time (see p.110), and these patterns are strung together to complete a 'song.' The basic beat of the song may range over a one- or two-bar pattern, and there may be variations written in for choruses, verses, middle eight and so on. Different patterns may also be needed for intros, outros, fills and breakdowns. (For more on song structure, see p.174.) And don't forget to record a pattern as a 'count-in' at the beginning of the piece.

A typical mid-priced machine may have sufficient memory to retain at any one time around ten songs and 100 patterns (depending on the complexity of the rhythms involved). Such information can be stored on the cassette and reloaded when required.

Most rock musicians — playing by ear — will write in real-time. First you choose a time signature and the bar length of your pattern — let's say two bars; then set the machine to start recording. A metronomic 'click' begins and will repeat itself every two bars. You simply tap in the beats using any sound setting you like until the rhythm is complete and to your satisfaction. As the two-bar cycle continues, you can put in more beats, or take them out. Furthermore — and this is the clever bit — the machine corrects the placing of the beats.

This function is called *quantizing*, and you can instruct the machine to quantize to the nearest quarter, eighth, sixteeth triplet, or to whatever accuracy you require. In practice, this makes life very easy: you can tap in the simple beats with a coarse quantization (say a quarter or eighth), then change to a fine quantization (say a 1/32nd triplet), to enable you to try your hand at something fancy. What's more, while tapping in the beats, you can slow the tempo right down, and bring it back up to speed for performance or recording.

With step-time programming, you need to write out or graphically to visualize the pattern. It is then tapped in one beat at a time as you step through, say, the sixteenth notes of each bar. To get a clearer idea of what's involved, here's an example of a simplified song. *(See Fig. 36)*

I tend to number my count-in pattern at 99, so I always know where it is and won't confuse it with any of the song patterns.

Humanizing the Machine

If you're a drummer coming to drum machines for the first time, you'll quickly discover that there are plusses and minusses to using them. It's great to be able to create perfectly executed patterns at the tap of a button; and to add all sorts of percussion to spice up your rhythms. But frustration may soon set in the moment you try to program a part you play live on the acoustic kit. Although you may be able to tap in the beats, somehow it doesn't *feel* quite right.

Rather, in the same way that the electronic kit is a different instrument from the acoustic kit, so the drum machine has to be treated as an instrument in its own right. It's often best to start off with the simplest rhythm that *works*, whether or not this is the rhythm you would play on a 'real' kit. Then you can judiciously begin adding parts without worrying about their 'playability.' You will gradually come to discover how to get the best out of your machine.

The better machines are touch sensitive or have programmable accent levels, so that it's possible to put dynamics into hi-hat patterns and drum fills. Careful use of quantizing on the more expensive machines will also help you to phrase fills and rhythms more naturally. Of course, mechanical rhythms are also great fun (check out everything from Dinosaur L to Prince to Erasure); it all depends on the style of music you play.

Performing With Machines

Drummers have always been called upon to keep good time. The invention of drum machines has made this even more crucial. By playing along with machines, most musicians, not least drummers, have discovered aspects of metronomic time and their relationship to it, of which they were previously unaware. On one level it's a pleasure to groove to a mechanical beat — here's a drummer that'll never let you down! But the beat is merciless. It doesn't bend; it doesn't deviate. And unless your own sense of timing is pretty good, your playing will make the machine part sound very stiff.

So, all musicians should now be very conscious of their timing. But for the drummer, things are more complicated. A drum machine may be used as the foundation for a song: the drummer may have to add to it, play over it, or replace it entirely when it comes to final recording or live performance. This requires careful listening and extremely accurate timing. Because of the sharp attack, fast decay and sheer volume of a drum beat, the slightest deviation by the drummer can be horribly noticeable.

It is therefore vital for drummers nowadays to practice playing to a drum machine or metronome, because this will help you become more aware of your weaknesses. Playing along to records is also useful. But it's easy to kid yourself that you're playing solidly and in time because you're hearing the drums on the record.

Fig. 36

SONG TITLE: TEMPO: $\quarternote$ = X beats per minute				SONG NO. 01 DATE:		
TIME	DESCRIPTION OF PART	PART NO.	PATTERN NO.	NO. OF BARS IN PATTERN	NO. OF REPEATS	TOTAL BAR COUNT
0min. 0 sec.	Count in Intro	1	99	2	1	–
		2	01	2		
		3	"	"	3	0
		4	"	"		
	Lead-In Verse I	5	02	2	1	6
		6	03	2		8
		7	"	"	4	
		8	"	"		
		9	"	"		
	Chorus I	10	04	2	3	16
		11	"	"		
		12	"	"	1	22
	End Chorus	13	05	2		24
		14	03	2		
		15	"	"	4	
		16	"	"		32
		17	"	"		
	Chorus Repeat and Fade	18	04	2		
		19	"	"	'n'	
		20	"	"		40
		21	"	"		
		22	"	"		
		23	"	"		
END	Song End					

Simplified Song Example

Cowbell

B.D.   S.D.   T.-t.   H.H.   Cabassa

open

Pattern 01
Introduction

"I think the new drum technology is fantastic because it gives us a chance to have access to some of the toys that keyboard players, guitarists and bassists have been enjoying for some years now. And because non-drummers are programming sequencers and drum machines, drummers have been forced to think differently about the way they use their instrument. So I don't think machines threaten acoustic drums at all; I think they add to what can be done musically."

OMAR HAKIM

Pattern 02
Lead-in

Pattern 03
Verse

Pattern 04
Chorus

Pattern 05
End of Chorus

Click Tracks

In the studio or on stage you may well have to play to a 'click' track. This might be a pattern you've programmed into a drum machine yourself, or it might be a sequenced rhythm or synth part fed to you from the keyboard player's set-up.

So, what makes a good click track? With a drum machine you could start with a simple four- or eight-to-the-bar pattern, including distinctive sounds like a handclap or cowbell, which will contrast with what you're playing on the kit. For the same reason, a syncopated pattern is often more comfortable to play with. But take care not to program something so complicated that you have no space left for your own kit part. The best place to start is to think of the most basic beat you're likely to play and to come up with the *simplest* syncopation against that.

Here are a few examples. These are great fun to play along with, as they immediately suggest dozens of possible rhythms. But treat them as rhythmic *outlines:* assign different sounds to different beats; add and subtract from the rhythm. Mess around with them!
(See Fig. 37)

The great advantage of a syncopated click is that it gives a better feel and is easier to groove with. A 'cold' metronomic click has no swing to it, and is more difficult to play with. You become overly aware of every beat, think too much about how you're playing, and stiffen up. It's therefore essential to be comfortable with whatever the machine or sequencer is feeding to you.

First of all, you must *hear* it. Insist on the monitor or headphone balance that you need. When recording, this is even more essential. You must stick with the machine track even if you can feel the guitarist or keyboard player pulling away from it. They're probably just doing a guide track and not concentrating too hard. But your head's on the block. So make a fuss. Get the guitar and keyboard lowered in the headphone mix!

Of course, much depends on whether the machine pattern is likely to become part of the finished track — in which case it must be programmed accordingly; and secondly, on how versatile the headphone mix is. If everyone's got the same mix, they're not necessarily going to appreciate hearing a four-to-the-bar cowbell loud enough to wake Quasimodo! In this situation, try a softer but busier pattern in eights or even sixteenths: something that's easy to keep track of.

"A lot of people ask me to play along with drum machines. In their pre-production they set up some drum machine patterns, sequence them, press a button and have their whole record there. And then they'd say 'Wow! We've got to liven this up with something — so let's have someone come in and do a hi-hat overdub or some cymbal crashes.' Also, I have to play a lot with click tracks in the studio. If they've got time code information down or they maybe want to overdub drum machine stuff later, then I would have to play along with the click and the click would be the main reference point for the whole record — triggering information, percussion, synth parts, sequences, all that kind of stuff."

OMAR HAKIM

"On a lot of records that I do, instead of having a busy kick and snare which tends to get in the way of the bass line and keyboard part, we use a lot of solid patterns but with the hi-hat dancing over the top. That makes the kick and the snare sound a lot more interesting, but doesn't take up so much space in the frequency spectrum of the record."

OMAR HAKIM

Fig. 37

Drum Machine "Click Track" Patterns

"In the studio, people find it hard to get a good balance and a good feeling with playing along to a click, and in the beginning it was a strange thing for me too. The first thing you think is 'Oh no—I can't hear it enough!'. But I've learned that when you go into a studio you have to make that environment as comfortable for you as possible, and never be afraid to ask for what is needed to get you there. Take your time. Get it right—'cos that's your work going down on tape, you know? So what I go for in the headphones is the feeling of a natural environment. I always ask the engineer to put some of that room tone in the mix, so that when I play it doesn't sound to me like I've got headphones on. It sounds like I'm playing drums in the room."

OMAR HAKIM

Drum Machines and Overdubbing

A common practice today is to overdub extra parts onto a machine-sequenced track to add color and sparkle to the rhythm. Machines are very good at the basic bass drum/snare drum pulse, which after all generally needs to be solid and consistent. The addition of *real* hi-hats, with their lighter touch, can make the track dance and skip more.

Because the bass drum and snare are machine-solid, it's possible to experiment with unusual hi-hat ideas — more spaced and angular, for example (see p. 90). And even while playing straight eights or sixteenths, the incorporation of accents or hi-hat open/closed patterns can make all the difference. *(See Fig. 38)*

With a sixteenths pattern, you may wish to leave a space where you'd normally play the snare. In this situation, you can find yourself thwacking your thigh on the snare beat. Be sure to cover it with a towel or cushion . . . Deaden the sound, not your leg!

Tom-Toms and Percussion

Having got a basic snare and bass drum pattern, it's useful to be able to leave tom-tom fills until later, when more of the song is recorded, and you can be more sure of getting the right fills in the right places. There are many ways of achieving this, but from the playing point of view, acoustic toms or electronic toms can really bring a

Fig. 38

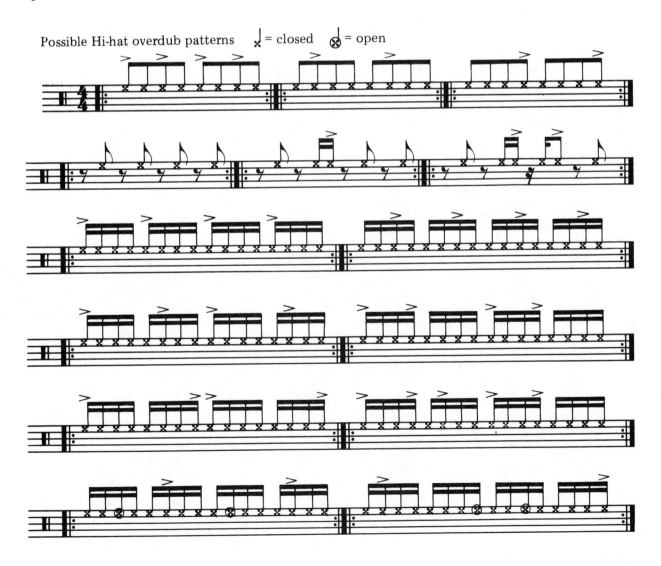

Possible Hi-hat overdub patterns ✗ = closed ⊗ = open

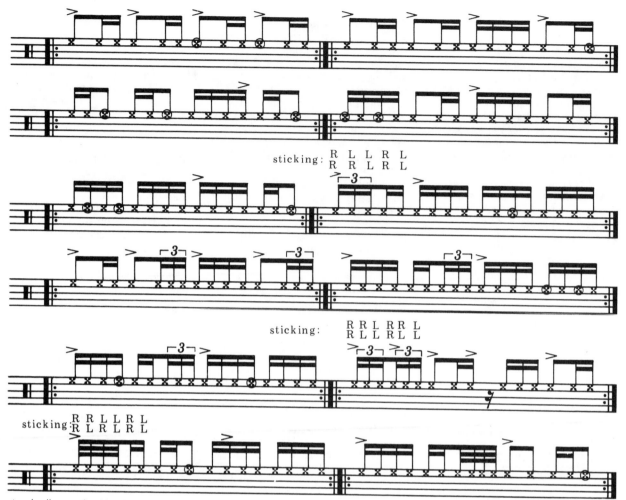

sticking:
R L L R L
R R L R L

sticking:
R R L R R L
R L L R L L

sticking:
R R L L R L
R L R L R L

track alive and add greatly to its dynamics. By weaving around the snare beat — or even removing a snare beat or two — you can give the impression of the toms being part of the original track, that is, played at the same time as the snare and bass drum parts. Alternatively, as with the hi-hats (see p. 91), playing over the top of the original pattern can give a dynamic lift while not interfering with the basic pulse.

Adding percussion is also a way to give a track sparkle. Drum machine-programmed percussion can be added in sync at any time, assuming that the machine is being sync'd from tape or used with a sequencer. In other words, the percussion can be added to the original song *patterns*. Or you can add percussion live, using the original instruments, or samples triggered from pads. An ideal combination for recording and live overdubbing, for example, is a set of Octapads linked to a Roland TR727 percussion machine, or to any machine with percussion samples stored on board.

PLAYING

A Word About Technique

In the most basic sense, playing a keyboard synthesizer is just the same as playing any other keyboard instrument: it's easy to sound *OK* pretty quickly. Unlike most stringed and wind instruments, the skill required to extract basic notes is minimal (your cat jumping on the note C won't make it sound vastly different from you playing the note C!).

While it's true to say that most synthesists start their musical life playing the piano or organ, this certainly doesn't have to be the case. Yes, the physical keyboards are identical, so of course a history of knuckle-rapping piano lessons is going to help, but today synth playing has far more to do with sounds, arrangement skills, and developing a general 'musical ear' than it ever has to do with flash manual dexterity.

Ninety per cent of a professional keyboard player's job is playing 'parts,' in other words finding lines,

riffs, chords, or effects that slot into — indeed make up — a complete song arrangement; and the success of these parts is down to two things: the sound, and the notes.

This may seem a blindingly obvious statement, but listen: a piano player or an organist is normally called upon to *play their instrument* throughout any particular performance. They learn the chords and the arrangement and then they play. . . . A synthesist is normally called upon to wear many hats: "Right, we want a sort of high string line here, then we want a deep growling noise there; we need a catchy little repetitive riff like a guitar in the chorus, and then we need a pad over the verse to provide some general background."

So how do you go about acquiring these many and varied skills? Well, seeing as synth playing is not simply about dexterity (though of course traditional keyboard skills come in handy), you can attack the problem at more than one level at a time. If you are just beginning to learn about keyboards and synthe-

Fats Domino

Ray Charles

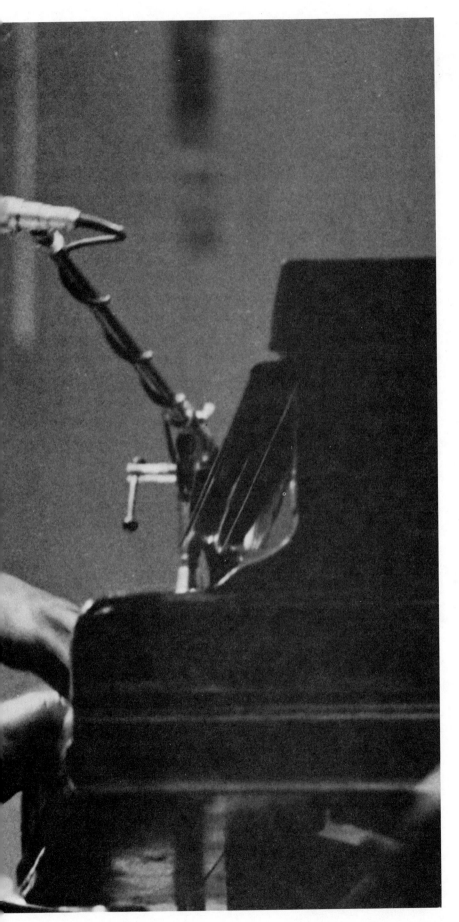

sizers, then divide your time equally between aquiring playing skills, aquiring programming skills (see p. 98), and learning about music in general. The 'complete synthesist' is one with imagination and knowledge in all three departments.

Basic Approaches to Keyboard Technique

There's no way I'm going to condense what can be a lifetime's work into a couple or paragraphs, but . . . if I can summarize keyboard playing, it is all about making life easy for yourself — relaxation.

The first thing to examine is the position of your hands on the keyboard. Ideally there should be something approaching a straight line from your elbow to your knuckles. Relax your fingers — they'll simply curl down towards the keyboard (see diagram below).

Sit up straight, and simply 'drum' your middle fingers over any three white notes, trying to make each note *sound*. Now try drumming them over five notes. Sound a total mess? OK, you need some practice!

General Fingering

You have two choices as a keyboard player: you can play individual notes or you can play chords. Both require some thought as regards fingering.

Fingering single notes: The whole point about fingering is to make your finger's movement from note to note as easy and painless as possible. In so doing you can then play what *you* want to play as opposed to what your fingers *allow* you to play. That's what it's all about.

There are few 'golden rules,' but quite a few 'guidelines.'

1. When playing a succession of single notes, avoid playing black notes with your thumb.

Alastair

Why not? It slides off easily! Your thumb is best employed as a kind of anchor, a focal point from which your fingers can do their bit safe in the knowledge of the thumb's whereabouts.

2. When playing a long succession of notes, you're going to have to move your arm up or down the keyboard. Try to keep your arm at right angles to the keyboard. Why? Because with *a straight wrist* your fingers can stay relaxed and ready for action. With too bent a wrist, your hand will become tense even before your fingers start moving.

3. When playing a run of notes that requires your thumb to be *tucked under*, do this as soon as your thumb has played its note. Why? Then it has time to play the next note smoothly and easily.

4. Think about what notes you want to play first, then think of how best to finger them. Why? Because it is all to easy

WAYS TO MAKE EXERCISING FUN

* Practice with a drum machine.
* Take any piece or passage that you enjoy playing, and transpose it into another key.
* Record yourself, hear your mistakes, learn from them.

for your fingers to fall into and play familiar shapes — simply because they are familiar, and not because they are the best notes to play. Work out what notes to play and then find the most logical route from one note to the next.

5. Avoid playing two successive notes using the same finger. Why? Because it can *only* sound jumpy. Even if this is the effect you want, you can create it by playing *staccato*, i.e., jumpily using different fingers.

6. Don't rely on the use of a sustain pedal to cover up the fact that you haven't worked out your fingering. This is such an easy trap to fall into. Work out problem passages without using the sustain pedal at all. Only then can you solve fingering problems.

Chord fingering

This is normally self-evident. Whether played in the left or the right hand, most chords can only (unless you're particularly perverse) be played using the 'correct' fingers.

However, many self-taught keyboardists seem to overlook the fact that they have *four* fingers, the little finger being the one most neglected. Don't. It is a valuable digit and one well worth exercising in order to get in shape.

When playing a *triad*, the most comfortable and normal fingers to use are the thumb, third finger (middle), and fifth (little finger) (see *Fig. 39*).

Problems creep in when, as one would expect to do from time to time, you have to move from·one chord shape to another. How do you do this smoothly?

Well, you can stamp on the sustain pedal if you like, but that's cheating! For smooth changes you have to employ a bit of cunning. If the notes of two chords are fairly near to each other (see *Fig. 40*), then the best way to move from one to the other is by sharing the workload, so to speak. For chord 1 use thumb, second and fourth finger. For chord 2 use

Fig. 39

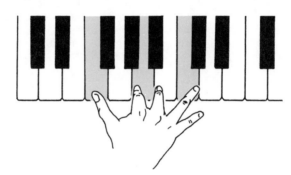

F Major

Fig. 40

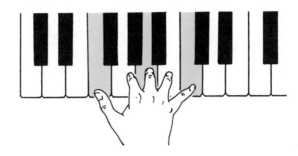

F Major

TO:

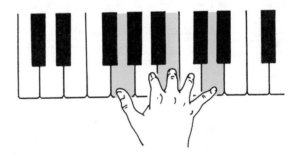

G Major

thumb, third and fifth finger. Play these two chords back and forth. Get used to the feel of it. Really only your thumb should move; your fingers should remain hovering over the keys.

Sometimes one is called upon to play a succession of chords that cannot be played using so simple a technique. For this you need to employ a very crafty technique used by organists (who don't have the luxury of a sustain pedal), which involves creeping from chord to chord by changing your fingering in midflight, so to speak.

Say you need to play a succession of triads based on

the C major scale, in other words C major, D major, E major, F major and so on. Play the triad of C major using thumb, second and fourth finger. Then play the triad of D major using thumb, third and fifth finger. Keeping this chord held down, switch your fingering from the third and fifth fingers to the second and fourth. Now you are free to play the next chord — E major — using thumb, third and fifth once again. And so on and so on.

Practice a whole octave's worth of this succession of chords — slowly and in time — then progressively speed up.

A FINGER EXERCISE YOU CAN DO WITHOUT A KEYBOARD:

Place your hands on a table-top, with your fingers curling down as if you were playing a keyboard. Lift up the fifth fingers — back from the knuckles — keeping your thumbs and remaining fingers on the table. Do this several times, then similarly lift up your fourth fingers, keeping thumbs and all remaining fingers on the table. Repeat for all fingers.

Exercises

Many people veer off into rock music having had a smattering of 'classical' training at school. And one of the prime reasons they do veer off is that they hate the rules and regulations, the sight reading, the theory, and the exercising!

However exercises do help. More importantly, and this point seems to have been totally overlooked by most 'classical' music teachers, they can be fun.

Why do we need exercises? For precisely the same reasons that athletes need them. They get you fit for the job in hand. Exercises help to provide you with manual skills that allow you to play what you *want* to play, and not simply have to trot out the same notes, riffs, or chord sequences — because they are the only one's you *can* play.

What particular skills are you trying to master?

1. Rhythm.

2. Strength — of fingers and wrists.
3. Independence — between fingers, and between left and right hands.

In short, exercises are stepping stones to freedom of expression.

Here are a few simple exercises to get you started. It doesn't really matter so much *what* you play as an exercise, just so long as you *do* exercise!

Fig. 41

Exercise for Stamina and Rhythm

Exercise for Finger Independence

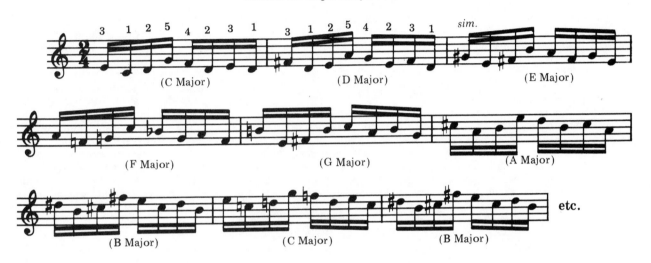

Exercise for Finger Strengthening and LH/RH Coordination

Synth Performance Controls

1. Pitch controller

The pitch controller is one of the synthesist's most expressive tools, allowing the player to change the pitch of notes or chords smoothly and progressively, in much the same way as guitarists do by bending strings.

How far notes can be 'bent' up or down depends on two things: the amount of physical movement of the controller, and the range you have programmed. Although on most synths you can set the range to bend up or down by one octave, a fifth up or down is generally accepted as the optimum range.

There are many different types of pitch controllers, and although

Guitarists, as we've seen, change pitch all the time. It's an integral part of guitar technique. But for keyboard players, the idea of using *both* hands in conjunction to produce *one* note may take some getting used to, especially if you're piano trained.

invariably a 'left hand' control, you can find them placed alongside the keyboard, just above, or sometimes stuck right at the top of the control panel. Surprisingly, it doesn't really matter where they are placed or which type they are (wheel — vertically or horizontally set, lever, ribbon, joystick . . .): all take a little getting used to for the novice.

Nothing sounds worse than misuse of the pitch controller (over or under bending, failing to return to basic pitch), so you need to feel comfortable with your instrument's particular type of controller and learn how to use it. The best way to practice is to work out a simple

brate' the controller as fast as you can, normally upwards. You may not need to do this if your synth possesses a modulation wheel.

Note bending is not only used for solo lines. It can be most effective with chords, especially at the beginning of a phrase, as in the following example:

(See Fig. 43)

How you operate a pitch *wheel* is largely a matter of taste, but by using the thumb (as opposed to a cluster of fingers/whatever gets there first!) you will be able to exercise greater control.

3. Portamento

This is a feature that produces a smooth pitch change between two played notes — as in the classic slow slide on a trombone. The only control, aside from on/off, is rate or speed, and this governs how quickly the note or chord changes from the first to the second played. A touch of portamento (i.e., very fast) can add interest to most solos, although many players currently feel that the effect does sound rather dated.

Glissando is a similar feature, though instead of a completely smooth transition between notes you will hear each distinct note in between. The effect is like running your thumb down the keys of the

It's also important to find a relaxed position for your pitch-bending hand — usually your left hand — so that your fingers don't get cramped.

riff or run — without using the pitch controller — and then substitute certain note changes for pitch bends (see *Fig. 42).*

If you feel you need more practice, try placing your right hand over the blues scale, say in C — the notes being **C, E♭, F, G, B♭.** Without moving the position of your fingers, try bending in and out of the secondary tones (or **passing notes**) of the scale. Holding your right hand steady on the principal notes will help you focus your attention on the pitch-bending side of your playing.

Pitch wheels can also be used to create vibrato effects. Simply 'vi-

2. Modulation controller

The modulation controller, normally a wheel or lever, merely acts as an amount or depth controller for the various types of modulation available on your instrument, as sent from the LFO. Its most common use is for vibrato.

Although the 'mod wheel' is not, in itself, as tricky to operate as a pitch controller, the two are best used in tandem — bend up to a high note in your solo and then add a touch of vibrato — and this can take a little practice. Try playing the following:

(See Fig. 44)

This controller can also be used for trills (set a square wave).

instrument — except that the black notes will also sound.

A thorough knowledge of your synth's performance controls together with a comfortable and relaxed approach to your keyboard playing are, of course, both vital to getting the sounds you want out of the instrument. However, you should also think long and hard about developing your *programming* skills as well. In the age of MIDI, step-time sequencing, quantizing, syncing, and sampling, no self-respecting musician can assume that a mastery of the keyboard equalling that of Rachmaninoff is by itself sufficient to get that all-important gig. (For more on programming, sequencing, etc., see pp. 101–113).

Modulation and/or pitch bending can be controlled by added key-speed or pressure on instruments whose keyboards respond to velocity or after-touch.

Fig. 42

Single Pitch Bend Up By One Tone

Normal

With pitch
bender

Play the note F and
bend up to the G

or "ornament" pitch bend-up and down one semi-tone
flip the bender up, then release it immediately

normal

with pitch
bend

* mordant: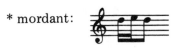

Fig. 43

Chord Pitch-Bending

Bend up to chord of Dm7 from one
tone below, so it sounds like:

Fig. 44

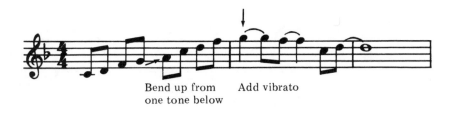

Bend up from   Add vibrato
one tone below

GUITAR, BASS, DRUMS TECHNIQUE UPDATE

Basic playing techniques for guitar, bass, and drums were covered in the companion volume to this book and in the first *ROCK-SCHOOL* TV series. But, partly because of the huge technological advances made in recent years, several new techniques have been developed which give guitarists, bassists and drummers access to new ranges of expression and style. These range from harmonics, to fretboard tapping, to 'open armed' drumming. It's time for an update.

pitch, are a whole series of overtones or *harmonics*, which consist of multiples of the basic frequency. You can play these harmonics by lightly touching a string with your left (fret) hand, picking the note with your other hand and simultaneously lifting your left hand away from the string to allow the harmonic to ring out. The strongest harmonic sound is to be found at the 12th fret (called the first harmonic); the next strongest at either the 7th or 19th fret (the second harmonic); and the next at the 5th fret (the third harmonic). Played in this way, you get the following notes: *(See Fig. 45)*

Using a trebly, distorted sound (and a bit of practice), you should be able to coax out harmonics at the fourth fret and just above the third fret as well:
(See Fig. 46)

The following patterns will enable you to build up whole scales, riffs and chords in harmonics. Take it very slowly at first and concentrate on your left (fret) hand position and coordination to help the harmonics really ring out.

This shows you how to play an E minor and B minor chord made up entirely of harmonics.
(See Fig. 47)

Fig. 45

Touch the strings *directly* over the fret

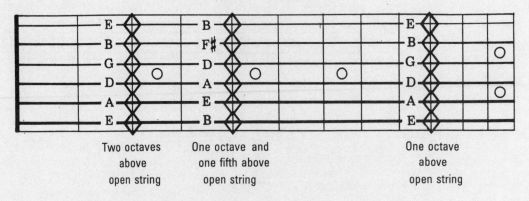

Two octaves above open string

One octave and one fifth above open string

One octave above open string

Fig. 46

GUITAR AND BASS

Harmonics
Harmonics enable you to extend your playing in many different directions. You can use them to add textures, creating soft bell-like sounds or chords — as does The Edge of U2; or you can use them with a harder, distorted sound to reach incredibly high notes well beyond the normal range of the guitar. Indeed, these harmonic 'screams' have been used to great effect by players like Jake E. Lee (Ozzy Osbourne), Brad Gillis (Night Ranger) and Steve Vai (David Lee Roth Band).

Open String Harmonics
When you pick a string, the main note or frequency that you hear is called the *fundamental*. Also present, but much quieter and higher in

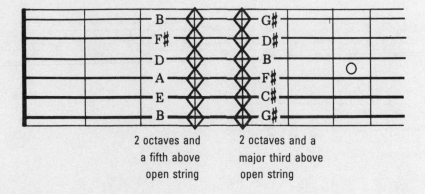

2 octaves and a fifth above open string

2 octaves and a major third above open string

Fig. 47

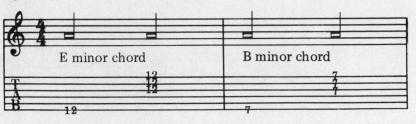

E minor chord

B minor chord

The Edge

This shows you the pattern of notes you get playing harmonics on just one string. The example here would sound good over an A major chord. When trying this pattern on different strings, bear in mind that the higher harmonics will be more difficult to play on the top strings.

(See Fig. 48)

This example illustrates a complete run that would sound good over an E minor chord.

(See Fig. 49)

You can find even more open string harmonic positions than those featured. But they're harder to play and softer in sound.

Fretted String Harmonics

A different approach, which is excellent for building up melodic patterns and chords, involves playing harmonics on fretted strings. There are two ways of doing this. The first is to tap hard with the right (pick) hand onto a fret exactly one octave above the fretted note held by your left (neck) hand, i.e., halfway between the fretted note and the bridge. Hold down a chord of G major and tap the strings as indicated in the diagram below:

(See Fig. 50)

Notice that you hear the fundamental and the first harmonic.

The second method has its origins in classical guitar technique and has been used to great effect by jazz player Lenny Breau and Police guitarist Andy Summers, among others.

Fig. 48

Fig. 49

Place the first finger of your right hand over the fret exactly one octave above the fretted note, so that it is lightly touching the string. Now strike the string either using a pick held between your thumb and second finger, or by plucking with your third or fourth finger.

By combining these harmonic techniques with echo, delay and chorus effects and a judicious use of the tremolo arm, you can send notes cascading and swooping all over the place. The audience will love it. Your keyboard player and vocalist may need some convincing though!

FRETBOARD TAPPING FOR GUITAR

Right Hand Hammer-Ons and Pull-Offs

In the first *ROCKSCHOOL* TV series and book we looked at how left (fret) hand hammer-ons and pull-offs could increase speed and fluency. Now we're going to look at some techniques using *both* hands on the fingerboard. This involves right (pick) hand hammer-ons and pull-offs.

These techniques have enabled guitarists to play rippling arpeg-

Fig. 50

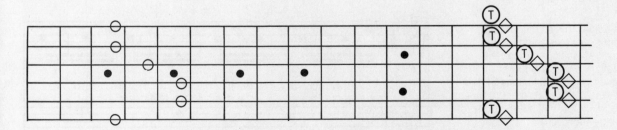

giated figures and wide intervals in a way that was once only possible on keyboards. Early exponents of this technique included Steve Hackett (then with Genesis) and Dickie Betts (then with The Allman Brothers). But the person responsible for popularizing it, and taking rock guitar to new heights, is Eddie Van Halen.

Before we go into detail, let's quickly have a look at left-hand hammer-ons and pull-offs, because tapping is basically a combination of the two but played by *both* hands.

A note is played by the right hand, while the string is fretted by the first finger of the left. The second or third finger of the left hand can then hammer down onto the string with enough force to create a second note (see *Fig. 51*).

Pick a note with the right hand in the usual way. The second or third finger of the left hand, meanwhile, 'flicks off' the string. This is done by pressing down hard onto a fret and then pulling the string down across the neck with enough force to sound the note fretted by the first finger of the left hand (see *Fig. 52*).

It's easier to use the first and second fingers to begin with, although it is possible to hammer-on and pull-off using the fourth finger. Try practicing combinations of 1-2/ 1-3/ then 2-3/2-4. You'll find that the fourth finger will need some extra attention.

Now let's go on to look at two-handed fretboard playing. Remember to take things slowly at first, to help build up evenly this new coordination between the left and right hands.

Find a convenient table-top or flat surface. Using the tips of the fingers, tap out a clear audible beat. Try to generate as much volume as possible *but do not use* the rest of the forearm for leverage. You'll find this hard at first — especially when using the third and fourth fingers. You should rest if your wrist or forearm begin to ache.

It's easier to use the first and second fingers to begin with, although it is possible to hammer-on and pull-off using the fourth finger. Try practising combinations of 1-2/ 1-3/ then 2-3/2-4. You'll find that the fourth finger will need some extra attention.

Now let's go on to look at two-handed fretboard playing. Remember to take things slowly at first to help build up evenly this new coordination between the left and right hands.

Find a convenient table-top or flat surface. Using the tips of the fingers, tap out a clear audible beat. Try to generate as much volume as possible *but do not use* the rest of the forearm for leverage. You'll find this hard at first — especially when using the third and fourth fingers. You should rest if your wrist or forearm begin to ache. *(See Fig. 53)*

Fig. 51

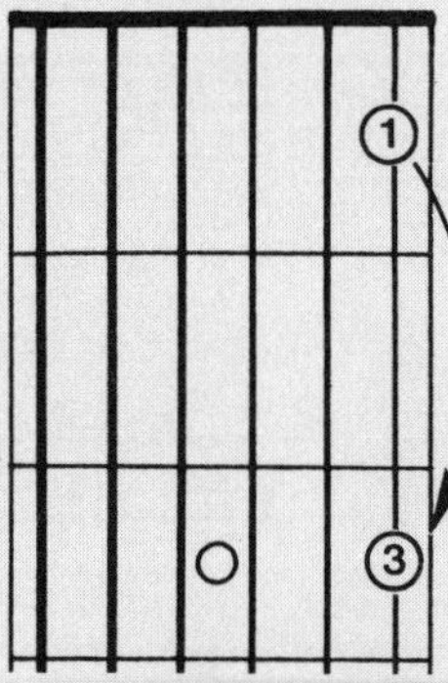

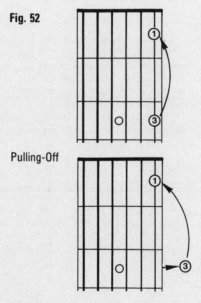

Hammering-On

Fig. 52

Pulling-Off

Fig. 53

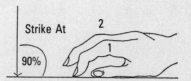

Strike At
2
1
90%

Once you feel comfortable with table-top tapping, try transferring it to the guitar. Balancing from the elbow, the forearm should be held inches above the strings, parallel to the guitar neck so that your hand is positioned comfortably over the notes that you want to play. As in the diagram above, the hand should be slightly arched to allow the tips of the fingers to point down onto the strings at right angles to the fretboard.

Now try tapping out the octave E and B at the 12th fret of the top E and B strings respectively. Using the first finger of the right hand, simply hammer-on the string until you can produce a clean note. Now let's try *tapping-off* (pulling-off with the tap finger).

Having tapped a note on the E octave, pull the string downwards away from you. At the crucial point, the E string will flick back, sounding a new note (in this case the open E, but it could be any note fretted by the left hand on that string).

Now do the same thing with the B string, still using the first finger of the right hand. Once you're comfortable, try tapping on and off both E and B strings consecutively, building up a fluid pattern. Use your left hand to prevent the open strings ringing on. Work at hitting the notes cleanly and accurately, because the strength of your fingers and the way they attack each note is crucial to the resultant sound.

Play a trill between the notes of A (fifth fret) and C (eighth fret) on the top E string with just your left (fret) hand (see *Fig. 54*).

Fig. 54

Eddie Van Halen

Now try to play the same trill using *both* hands, as follows: *(See Fig. 55)*

While the left hand first finger anchors the A note, the right hand taps down firmly on the string at the eighth fret, hammering on a C note; then bring your finger off the string, moving slightly sideways so that you pull off and in so doing sound the lower note. Keep repeating the process until you build up a fluid trill.

Try tapping this phrase with your *second* finger as well. You will then have the option of holding a pick between your thumb and first finger so that you can quickly switch between picking and right hand tapping.

The next example involves using

Fig. 55

right and left hand hammering-on and pulling-off to build up an arpeggiated figure of A minor. *(See Fig. 56)*

The fourth example is very similar to the last, but this time you end up playing an arpeggio of A major. *(See Fig. 57)*

In the next example, the right (pick) hand taps a melody by moving alternately from the 12th to the 10th fret, while the left hand hammers on between the fifth and eighth fret. *(See Fig. 58)*

Try these first three examples on all the strings of the guitar, one after another, and work out which broken chords you're playing.

Fig. 56

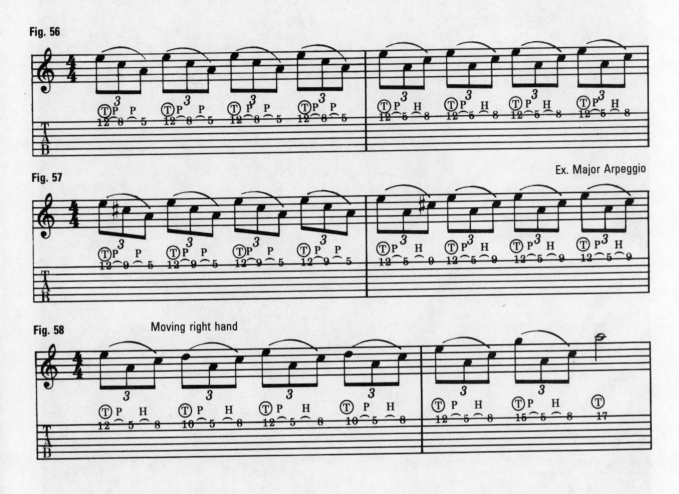

Ex. Major Arpeggio

Fig. 57

Fig. 58   Moving right hand

Now here's an example similar to the one above, but more adventurous. The right hand taps a melody by moving between several frets on the G string, while the left hand ends up hammering-on between the fifth and ninth frets — quite a wide stretch if you're not used to it. (See Fig. 59)

Fig. 59

Adrian Belew

Here are two examples involving the use of *open* strings. *(See Fig. 60)*

Fig. 60

Now let's try combining string bending with right hand tapping. *(See Fig. 61)*

Fret a C on the third (G) string with the first finger of your left hand. Pick the string and then hammer on a D using the left hand third finger. With the right hand tap on an octave G at the 12th fret. Then bring the G up to A by *bending the string using the left hand.*

Pick a C and hammer on a D as above. With your left hand, bend the D up to E. If you tap on at the 12th fret now, you will get a high A. *(See Fig. 62)*

Repeat this procedure, but, having tapped on at the 12th fret, slide your right hand to the 14th fret. Remember to hold the left hand bend while doing this. The end result is a C hammered-on to D, bent up to E, with a tapped-on high A slid up to B. *(See Fig. 63)*

This last example incorporates right and left hand pulls and hammers, and right hand slides. Notice that although the complete riff contains 12 notes, you only pick the *first* note. *(See Fig. 64)*

Fig. 61

Incorporating String Bending

Fig. 62

Fig. 64

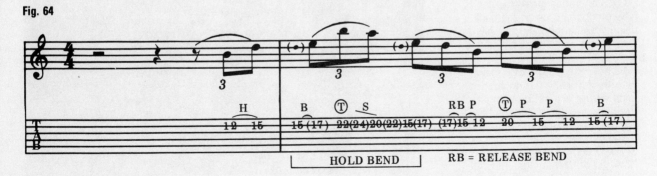

TWO-HANDED BASS PLAYING

Sounds silly, doesn't it? After all, everybody already plays bass using two hands. But a new and exciting technique has been developed by guitarists in recent years that involves creating sounds by the force of the fingers of *both* hands hammering down on the fretboard (see p.134). This idea is now being adapted by bassists. But because of the weight of the strings and the different size of frets and neck, the bass tapping technique is slightly different.

Having loosened up the first and second fingers of your right hand with the table-top exercises described on p.134, position your right hand over the top end of the neck in the same way as for guitar. Now try tapping out the octave G and D at the 12th fret of the G and D strings respectively. Using the second and first fingers of the right hand, simply hammer-on the string until you can produce a clean note. Now let's try *tapping-off* (pulling-off with the tap finger).

Having tapped a note on the G octave with the second finger, pull the string sideways towards the D string. At the crucial point, the G string will flick back, sounding a new note (in this case the open G, but it could be any note fretted by the left hand on that string). The tap finger finally comes to rest on the adjacent string.

Now do the same thing with the D string, this time using the *first* finger of the right hand. Once you're comfortable, try tapping on and off both G and D strings consecutively, building up a fluid pattern. Think of your right hand as tapping *and* plucking the strings. Use your left hand to prevent the open strings ringing on. Work at hitting the notes cleanly and accurately, because the strength of your fingers and the way they attack each note is crucial to the resultant sound.

OK, congratulations! You can now produce notes on the neck using your right hand. Let's have a look now at ways of applying this technique.

Hold down the chord of F major with the left hand. Using your right hand, strum across the strings from low to high. While the harmony is still ringing out, tap on the A and D notes at the seventh fret of the D and G strings respectively. Now tap off the strings and you'll hear the F and A notes from the chord. (See *Fig. 65*).

It's possible to build up a rippling arpeggio effect by first strumming the chord and then tapping the extra notes on and off in rapid succession. You can also move the tapped notes around and change the chord shape underneath. See how many variations you can come up with.

Fig. 65

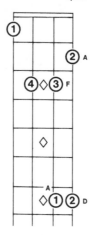

Extending Chords

Left and Right Hand Neck Combinations

Left hand hammer-ons and pull-offs can be followed by right hand taps on the same string. Playing in a steady eighths rhythm, for example, hammer on a C at the fifth fret of the G string, followed by a pull-off to B. Now pull off the B to the open G string followed by a right hand tap onto the octave G at the 12th fret. Now tap off the octave G onto the fretted C. Keep the cycle going and try to increase your speed and fluidity (see diagram below). Keeping the same hand position, transfer this example first to the D string and then to the A. After that, try experimenting with new combinations of notes.

Stanley Jordan

Once upon a time, a bass player's right hand only had to worry about *plucking* notes; now it has to cope with tapping, slurring and sliding too!

Fig. 66   (fingering)

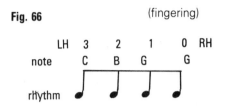

(All notes are played on the G string)

Here's another example. With the left hand, fret a C on the G string. After plucking the note, hammer on the D with the third finger, followed by the E♭ with the fourth finger. Tap on the octave G with the second finger of the right hand. Now tap off the octave G to sound the E♭, pull off the left hand fourth finger to sound the D, and finally pull off the left hand third finger to sound the C. Again, this cyclical phrase can be built up to enormous speeds.

Tapping Extra Notes

Tap an octave G at the 12th fret of the G string. Keeping the finger depressed, slur it back and forth between the octave G and the F two frets below it. Do it again, but this time slide up to the A two frets above the octave G. Aim for a smooth movement and experiment with different finger pressures until you're comfortable. With practice, you should find it possible to slide up to A and then to the B above the octave G, all with one tap-on.

Here are two examples combining right hand tapping and slurring with left hand hammering-on.

Using steady eighths as a basic pulse, fret a D note with the first finger of the left hand at the seventh fret of the G string. With the right hand second finger, tap on the octave G, sliding up to A and then to B. Tapping-off the string at B will produce the sound of the fretted D again. With the third finger of the left hand, now hammer on an E. By tapping-on a G once more, you can repeat the cycle. Do you recognize it? It's the major pentatonic scale.

Here is a six-note pattern that incorporates the open G string (see diagram below):
(See Fig. 67)

Hammer on the fourth finger of the left hand. Pull off to the second, then to the first and then to the open G string. With the right hand, tap on the F at the 10th fret, slurring up to the octave G, and then tap off the octave G to the left hand fourth finger, sounding the D in the process.
(See Fig. 68)

Convert both these patterns to the minor key. And remember that any of these finger positions can be moved to another string to create a new key, although it does get harder to produce volume and attack with the thicker strings.

Left and Right Hand Hammers Combined

Using the low E and A strings, hammer on a G and D at the third and fifth fret respectively, with the left hand first and third fingers. Follow this by tapping a high E and A at the 14th fret on the D and G strings, using the second and first fingers of the right hand. (See diagrams — *Fig. 69*.)

Fretboard tapping like this can open up a whole new means of expression to the adventurous bass player. Get out there and do it!

Fig. 67

G open string)

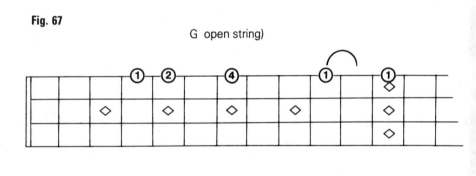

Fig. 68

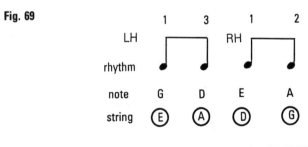

Fig. 69

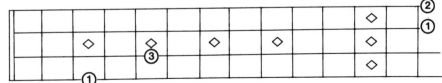

DRUMS

New Styles and Coordinations

Because drum machines have no limitations on their technique or 'coordination,' and because they're often programmed by songwriters or producers — musicians who are not necessarily drummers — some records have drum parts that are either 'impossible' to play or that challenge the drummer to come up with new playing techniques.

How does this come about? Often a programmer will start with a basic bass drum/snare drum pattern. A live drummer would almost certainly find a ride or hi-hat pattern to lock such a pattern together. But a machine snare/bass pattern is so solid, especially if it's sequenced with a keyboard or bass riff, that there's often no immediate need for a hi-hat. So a broken-up or 'difficult' hi-hat pattern may be added, or hi-hats combined with

percussion or maybe tom-tom sounds. And beats can be added or subtracted without needing to worry about the difficulties of live duplication.

To help match the feels of such patterns live, one approach is to play a simple snare drum/bass drum pattern and to use the hi-hat to play rather more sparse and syncopated patterns. Remember to keep a good flow going, though. A few examples are shown below.

Styles and Coordinations: Syncopated Hi-Hats

Fig. 70

To strengthen the left hand and increase control:
Practice the rudiments and different sticking control patterns;
Play all your rhythms leading with the left hand as well as with the right.

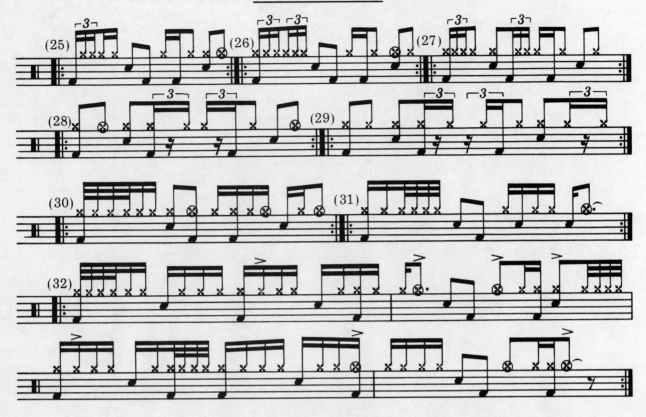

In these examples, the hi-hat is at first sparse and broken up. Gradually it becomes fuller as the eighths and sixteenths reappear, but in a syncopated fashion. At this point, try also the hi-hat patterns from p.119 over the bass drum/ snare drum patterns of the present examples. Finally, you come to example 36, which is based on the feel of Omar Hakim's playing in program two of the *ROCKSCHOOL* TV series.

This expansion of coordination and rhythm is reflected in other techniques that imply a more *ambi-dextrous* approach to kit drumming, making a more extensive use of the left (or weaker) hand and foot.

Billy Cobham has been demonstrating an ambidextrous approach to jazz and rock drumming for many years. As well as playing a conventional right hand ride cymbal, he leads with the left on the hi-hat or on a second ride cymbal set up to the left of the kit. The result is a distinctive 'open-armed' playing style. A new generation of brilliant players, including Simon Phillips, uses similar techniques to great effect. I've already mentioned Gary Chester's exploration of this approach (see p.92). Part of his teaching is to practice every rhythm leading with the left as well as the right.

There are other ways of making the left hand more effective, which are becoming increasingly popular. For example, the following rhythms are all based on one idea: to play a familiar pattern using just the left (or weaker) hand, rather than both hands. The basic pattern is as follows: *(See Fig. 71)*

Fig. 71

Now just see how many variations you can make from it:

Fig. 72

Billy Cobham

This is just one way of making the left hand more effective. As the later examples show, the basic pattern can be elaborated upon, introducing double hi-hat beats, and so on. Eventually, you get rudimental patterns between the hi-hat left hand and the ride cymbal right hand. And this opens up a whole new area for rhythmic invention, an area in which Steve Gadd has been inspirational over the past decade.

It's also a good reason to go exploring and practicing the rudiments and sticking variations! This is too big an area to go into in any detail here, so one example will have to suffice: *(See Fig. 73)*

If you try the same approach with the feet, this will help you to use double bass drums (or a double bass drum pedal), and will also

help left foot hi-hat facility. Opening and closing the hi-hat accurately while playing sixteenth note patterns with the hands requires good control.

Finally, when playing on the ride cymbal with the right hand, different left foot rhythms can be played on the hi-hat to suggest different feels. Practice all your rhythms using the following four hi-hat variations: *(See Fig. 74)*

Fig. 73

Fig. 74

4 Vocal Techniques

Aretha Franklin

Annie Lennox

Introduction

The voice is the most flexible, most expressive and most important instrument in music. Everyone can sing. And the success and popularity of rock in particular is due to that fact. We can all sing along. Having said that, the demands of fronting a band are such that not everyone can *perform*. Most full-time rock vocalists have developed a whole catalogue of skills, exercises and routines designed to protect the voice, extend its range and power, and generally make it sound the way you want to hear it. Some take lessons. Most learn the hard way.

Singing, of course, is the one area of music where the basic technology involved has not been supplanted by the microchip. It all still depends on how you use the lungs, throat, nose and mouth you were born with! Nevertheless, there are one or two things you have to bear in mind. First off, you've got to consider adapting your voice to amplification and effects. While on stage, you might not *feel* that your voice is a part of you — it'll be coming from the P.A., from monitor speakers or side-fills — a disconcerting experience if you're not used to it. And most important of all, you have to learn to work with a microphone — a close friend you can whisper to or shout at depending on your mood.

Remember, too, that performing as a vocalist involves learning about expression and dynamics, both of which stem from a control of your breathing and your posture. And perhaps most important of all, you have to think about *protecting* your voice from the rigors of constant performance.

So, where do you start? Well, over the next few pages we're going to look at basic vocal and microphone techniques, simple ways of protecting the voice, phrasing, dynamics, vibrato and a few hints at harmonies and arrangements. And, as there's no substitute for experience, *ROCKSCHOOL* producer Chris Lent went out and talked to a number of leading vocalists from different fields — Graham Bonnet of Alcatrazz, Midge Ure of Ultravox, blue-eyed soul man Michael McDonald, and Juliet Roberts of UK jazz-soul outfit Working Week. Their conversations are printed below.

Bryan Ferry

G. Bonnet

ALCATRAZ SOLITARY

British singer Graham Bonnet possesses one of the finest and most enduring voices in rock. As front-man for Australian group *The Marbles* in the late '60s, he caught the public's attention with his soulful rendition of "Only One Woman," an international hit for the band.

After working on various projects in Australia, Graham joined megawatt supergroup *Rainbow*, helping Ritchie Blackmore's outfit to produce a classic LP ("Down to Earth") and a couple of smash singles ("Since You've Been Gone," "All Night Long").

Following a brief and rocky stint with ace German axeman Michael Schenker in 1982, Graham moved to California and formed West Coast rabble rousers *Alcatrazz*, whose albums ("No Parole From Rock'n'Roll," "Disturbing The Peace," "Dangerous Games") feature a level of vocal and lyrical sophistication not often heard in hard rock. (Check out tracks like "God Bless Video," "Will You Be Home To-night," "That Ain't Nothing," "Shooting Star".) Clearly Graham Bonnet is a man with a lot to say on the art of vocalizing. . . .

CL: How did you develop the range and power of your voice?

GB: When I was a kid, instead of singing pop songs like most kids did, I used to listen to people like Mario Lanza, and when I was about seven I remember walking around singing with this big voice — a little kid with a big voice — and it amused my parents so I kept it up. And when I got a little older, instead of singing guys' songs, I used to sing along to the Crystals and the Ronettes in *their* key, so that opened up my voice a lot. I used to sing the high notes in full voice and that sort of helped me build my stomach muscles up to get it really pumping out.

CL: You've never taken singing lessons or anything like that?

GB: No. I was born into a very musical family. My mum sang, my brothers sang in the choir, my uncles play instruments — all that kind of stuff. So Christmas time was like show time; everybody got out their trumpet or accordion or whatever and everybody sang. That's where it came from originally.

CL: Do you think singing lessons would be a good idea for vocalists?

GB: Yeah — even for me! For example, I know that sometimes I'm probably breathing incorrectly and I'm singing the wrong way because my voice *does* go. It's hard to say why it goes, but I think I could still do with lessons. You never stop learning. So maybe I'll go to a tutor who'll teach me how to breathe properly and run around the stage at the same time, because that's the hard part!

CL: Have you ever had problems with your throat at all?

GB: When I was about 20 I had nodes, which was probably from drinking. I used to drink scotch a lot and it really burnt my throat right out, and I had to stop talking for about two months. Luckily they never came back.

CL: Can you tell us a bit about getting in shape for singing, protecting the voice, especially when you're on tour?

GB: Well, your lungs have to be in good shape for a start because that's what starts the whole thing — the air obviously — and your muscles have to be in good shape. If I've been off the road for a while I really ache from singing during rehearsals. But it soon comes right! On the road, of course — well, you're in a rock'n'roll band, and it's a rock'n'roll life so it's really hard to be Mr. Perfect. But I can tell you what I try to do. I don't drink too much and I always make sure I sleep enough and eat the right things, which is very hard on the road sometimes because I'm a vegetarian. And I know that I should never have a beer or anything before going on stage because it really makes you dehydrate and then your voice disappears. So normally I drink water on stage and

Crystals

Ian Gillan

use a throat spray. And when I'm at home between tours I exercise a lot. I go running with my dog and sing at the same time. And that helps build up my lungs.

**CL: I can understand the thing about not drinking alcohol, but
I've heard that *milk* is also a problem . . .?!**

GB: Yeah — milk is the worst thing. It really puts a lousy slimy coat of grease on your vocal cords. I remember a London throat specialist saying to me, don't drink whisky or any hard liquor — and I thought, okay — but whatever you do don't drink milk, because that

will ruin your voice for the whole day. It really sticks there and makes your mouth all smacky and funny and other horrible things come out — well anyway, I won't talk about that. It's not very nice.

CL: I wonder if we could get some advice from you about vocal technique. You're our teacher for the day!

GB: I find that when I sing bass parts, bass harmonies or something, the best way to sing it is to bring your head right up. It's like being a sword swallower, you know, and that's the only way to do it because then the throat is open . . . and, well, it's a pipe after

all and if the throat is open then the note can come out easier than if you tilt your head down and screw the throat up. For high notes, I find it better to keep my head straight. And generally I like to mess around with stupid noises (*sings "Deooo!"*) and that kind of thing really warms you up even though it might sound stupid. And another thing I should do but don't is to let the jaw drop to relax the throat before a session. You look like an idiot, but it's just something you do!

CL: A lot of people starting out in bands, especially playing heavier music, find that when

G. Bonnet

G. Bonnet

they actually get to performing, it's quite a strange experience to sing in front of a megawatt backline. What would your advice be in terms of finding your notes?

GB: It's basically really hard to keep in tune with guitarists nowadays because they're bending strings and one thing and another. So what I usually do is with Jimmy (*Waldo, ex-keyboard player with Alcatrazz*), I have him really loud through my monitors, like you wouldn't believe. I have him as loud as I have myself, because the keyboards are pretty constant pitchwise. So that's how I tune. But there have been nights when I can't hear anything and I've had to pitch to the bass drum!

CL: Let's talk a bit about expression and vibrato.

GB: In rock'n'roll you never use your real voice. You never use the whole body — it's always half of what's really there, because if you used the whole thing you'd sound ridiculous, like an opera singer, which is wrong for this style. So you have to cut it down. It's more croony, if you like. Rock'n'roll isn't as heavy as a lot of people try to make out. I use a lot of different voices. I have probably three or

Otis Redding

Sam Cooke

four voices that I use on our records anyway. On certain songs, like "Only One Woman," for example, it's like a sob song, and for that it always helps if your throat is just a little bit tight, because it gives a feeling of someone who's just been crying, a kind of soul feeling. I remember when I recorded that, the producer wanted me to sound a little rough, a touch of the Otis Reddings, because Otis Redding always had that thing like he'd just been crying his heart out over something, and it made it sound soulful. So that's one kind of voice I use. Now with vibrato, I usually use it to sweeten the end of a note (*sings "God Bless Video"*). But I don't like to use too much. In fact I've been trying to cut down on my vibrato. It becomes very addictive, you know.

CL: What are the role of vocals in Alcatrazz and how is it different perhaps from other heavy rock outfits?

GB: We base a lot of our songs around the vocal, whereas in past versions of Alcatrazz, a lot of the songs were written around the guitar. On the album we've just recorded (*"Dangerous Games"*) we went out of our way to feature the leads vocal and to bring in harmonies — sometimes with the other guys in the band and sometimes me overdubbing myself. So we're still a heavy rock band, but also vocal, which most bands aren't.

CL: How do you actually work out your harmonies?

GB: Well, if it's just for me I work them out on my guitar, you know — find the root note and work up from there, or just listen and it comes naturally. And then other times, when we work it out with the band together, we just mess around in the studio until we get a good blend of voices, because some guys have louder voices than others, and some guys sing higher better than others; even though they can't really sing high, it makes it sound better if they push it that little bit extra. So we really sort of work it out between us.

THINGS TO REMEMBER

1. Relaxation is the key to good vocals. Work out ways of relaxing the throat, chest and shoulders.
2. Breath control is vital — so get your lungs in good shape. Go jogging if you have to!
3. Drink water on stage or in the studio. Alcohol will dry up your throat; milk will gum it up (although some singers say that *warm* milk helps to relax the throat).

Juliet Roberts

WORKING OUT

Juliet Roberts fronts hot UK jazz-soul band *Working Week*. With a voice distinctive for its range of expression and power, Juliet has rapidly established herself as one of Britain's foremost young singers — as sessions with Loose Ends, Owen Paul, Stephen 'Tin Tin' Duffy, Junior, and James Ingram all testify.

After working with various bands in and around her native West London, she joined Working Week in 1984, providing them with a vocal focus and onstage presence that has stood them in good stead on British and European tours (check out "Shot in The Dark" and "It's All Over Now," for example). We spoke about basic technique, enunciation, phrasing, and pacing yourself.

CL: What tips could you give on basic vocal technique?

JR: Well, posture is really important. I had problems with that because basically I am a sloucher. A good exercise to overcome this is to stand up straight, raise both hands up above your head and bring them slowly back down by your sides, relaxing the shoulders at the same time. The way you end up standing is the ideal posture for singing. Breathing correctly is also vital. I try to think I'm blowing into a balloon. That usually helps. Pitch, of course, is something to work on. You could try playing a note on a keyboard or guitar and harmonizing to it — singing, say, a third or a fourth — just to get your ear used to harmony.

CL: Do you think it's a good idea for vocalists to learn a bit about music?

JR: Yes — it can improve your pitching and tuning. I mean, I used to play trumpet. It was one of my father's ideas, actually. He said all vocalists should play a wind instrument to help with their breath control. I couldn't believe he wanted so much noise around the house! He had me doing trumpet, my sister on trombone, my brother on clarinet — and we all sang as well. He really wanted us to learn, I guess. But it was great training. Because now I've got pretty good pitch. For example, I can hit a G or a C straight off automatically (*sings*).

CL: What about enunciation and phrasing?

JR: Certain vowel sounds can cause you to put an unnecessary strain on the throat if you sing them as you speak them. E is the classic example. Your mouth goes right across and throws all the logic of how you're supposed to sing out of the window, because your mouth is supposed to go *downwards* to let the air out. Now my vocals coach (Helena Shanell) advised me to *darken* the vowels, to think of rounder sounds. So with 'e,' you think of pronouncing it like 'i' as in 'bin.' And that makes your mouth go down and everything at the back of your throat widen.

As far as phrasing is concerned, I try to mimic other people's voices off records. For fast stuff, like Manhattan Transfer, I used to slow the records down, get the part off pat and then work up to it. Obviously, the more you sing it yourself, the more you put your own expression into it. I remember that with one Patti Austin album, I didn't copy the way she sang so much as the way she *breathed*. I learned a lot about phrasing that way. And even now when tackling a new tune I might think 'how would Patti sing this?' Or Anita (Baker), or Chaka (Khan), or whoever. I also used to tape myself singing along to records. That can be a big shock. It can reveal all kinds of weaknesses, from phrasing to pitching!

Patti Austin

Anita Baker

CL: Aren't the basic characteristics of different rock vocal styles due — or at least partly due — to differences in phrasing?

JR: Yeah — there are always little extras that go into making a certain style. Hard rock is often very staccato, the melody based around one note. Reggae might use nursery rhyme tunes, very sort of twee with a call-and-response backing vocal. Soul is very melodic, lots of frills and embellishments. Country and Western might be more like a blues song with a bit of soulfulness thrown in.

CL: You can, of course, mix and match these different characteristics.

JR: Rock songs, over the last five years especially, have been using wonderful soul backing vocals and gospel harmonies. I mean Foreigner's "I Want to Know What Love Is" — that is a classic rock song. It sounds like a football chant, but with this massive black gospel choir going on, which is brilliant. So now the whole thing's been fusioned together and I think that's good, really.

CL: How conscious are you of 'placing' the voice?

JR: In the chest or head or whatever? To a certain extent, I suppose. When I'm singing, I tend to think more about the sound than the actual notes. So I'll think 'down' for a deep note and it'll go down to the chest. Or for really nasally sounds — which are so unlike my natural voice anyway — I might have to play around a bit more, trying to focus my voice into the

Chaka Khan

back of the throat or the roof of my mouth. But a lot of the time I place it very straight in the throat and chest, because that's where the sound comes from, basically.

CL: Relaxation seems to be one of the keys to good singing — and yet it must be hard to relax on stage in front of an audience. How do you cope with this?

JR: You should never be shy about singing. As a kid I used to sing everywhere — at school in the drama class, in the church choir. I was a bit of a show-off actually. But it meant that singing became natural to me. So I do get butterflies sometimes before going on stage but I'm never nervous — not about having to sing, anyway. One thing that helps me to relax and to warm up my voice is to sing along to a tape in the dressing room before the show. I usually sing low songs, sung by men with mellow voices — maybe Luther Vandross, Stevie (Wonder), The Gap Band — stuff like that. Then maybe I'd go onto something in a higher register — early Rufus, perhaps. I've actually got a collection of tapes that I take on tour with me. By the time I'm ready to go on stage I'm trying a few high notes just to make sure I've gone all the way up as far as I can. But you know, it's just a question of taking it slowly and sensibly, starting at the bottom of my range and working up to the top and getting the throat and chest relaxed and ready to go.

A lot of it depends on the set as well. The first song we do is "Shot in the Dark," and I'm always very aware of what's going on: the audience, my pitch, and the sound of my voice — because it changes from day to day. And then we do "I Thought I'd Never See You Again," which is a mid-tempo song. That's when I start to get ev-

Luther Vandross

erything into perspective. My voice might be a little bit tired that night, so I compensate. I don't rush things and take my time getting to it. Another night everything might be going good, and you think 'my voice can take it' — so you batter it to death. But a lot of this is automatic. After the first couple of songs I'm usually more worried about tripping over the bass player's lead!

CL: In fact isn't it possible to get too self-conscious about all this?

JR: Absolutely. Sometimes I find myself trying to sound too correct and I lose the feeling in my voice. When I began with Helena (Shanell — UK voice tutor), I saw her non-stop for a couple of months. Then when I did a new song with the band, I sang it *so* correctly — it was disgusting. It had no feeling. I had lost all the soul, all the heart, and everyone said 'great — next time we want an opera lesson, we'll call you!!' So now I try to incorporate all the advice and training I get from Helena with the natural roughness and edge that I have.

THINGS TO REMEMBER

1. Enunciation and phrasing are as important as breath control; watch out for certain vowel sounds — 'darken' and round out the thinner vowels like 'a' and 'e,' so your mouth opens downwards.
2. Listening to records and tapes can help you with your phrasing, vocal style, ear and timing; slow down the track if necessary; listen to *all* aspects of the vocal, including the breathing!
3. When performing, think about the pacing of your set; vary the highs and lows in terms of pitch, range and tempo, to avoid over-stretching the voice.
4. Don't be shy about singing; but don't become so self-conscious about technique that you lose all feeling and soul; a good vocal technique is only there to help *release* your vocal personality, not to trap it.

Midge Ure

VOX POP

Ultravox frontman Midge Ure is a man of many parts: vocalist, songwriter, guitarist, producer. His career is equally varied, including stints with tartan teenyboppers *Slik* and New Wave hopefuls *The Rich Kids*, before joining Ultravox in 1980.

Midge's dynamic and dramatic voice fits perfectly into the often Gothic grandeur of the Ultravox sound. Tracks like "Vienna," "Visions in Blue," "Hymn," and more recently "All Fall Down," illustrate a vocal style that ranges from breathy and intimate to soaring and intense.

In 1986, Midge released a solo album, "The Gift," containing classy pop tunes like "If I Was," "When The Wind Blows," and a reworking of *Jethro Tull's* "Living In The Past." Lighter in vein than much of Ultravox, "The Gift" nevertheless displays a voice as versatile and polished as ever.

We spoke firstly about singing on stage, and using technology to support the voice . . . .

CL: What can you tell us about microphone technique?

MU: The quieter and lower the voice, the closer you tend to be to the mike. For higher and louder notes, you should move back to keep the sound levels comfortable. So you've got to *know* when you're going to sing loud and back off accordingly. Another thing you can do when reaching the end of a powerful high note — as the note starts to fade away naturally — is to come back into the mike. again, so the microphone is acting like a volume control on your voice and can give the impression that the voice is much more powerful than it really is.

CL: When you're working close to the mike, don't you have problems with breath noise, popping and so on?

MU: In live work you don't really hear that too much. Most people, when they're performing live, you actually see them with their lips pressed right against the microphone and it's simply because the closer they are to the mike, the better they're going to hear themselves through the monitors. There's always a monitoring problem when you're performing live. But in a studio it's very different. The engineer will make you stand a reasonable distance away from the microphone to stop all the pops and noises and clicks and things that you get naturally.

CL: When you're working on stage with monitors do you — or did you when you were first starting out — find it a disorientating experience to hear your voice coming not from you, but from somewhere else?

MU: It *is* a bit odd. But I seem to remember that just the joy of having monitors instead of trying to hear what was coming out of the PA alone — because in the early days we just didn't have monitors — the joy of actually having monitors overcame any disorientation that you'd normally get. There is something a bit strange about sining into a piece of metal and hearing it come out of a wooden box on the floor or at the side of the stage, whereas when you're sitting in your bedroom just strumming your guitar and you're singing away, you're hearing your voice from inside the room, and you're hearing it inside your head. But when you've got loud music on

stage, you don't hear any of that at all. You've got to depend on a good monitoring system.

CL: Getting away from microphones and amplification for a moment, let's talk about general vocal techniques and arrangement. How important, for example, is breath control to you?

MU: Take a song like "If I Was" (*from Midge's solo LP "The Gift"*) — on that particular track it is very important, because the words are all strung together. There's a lot of lyric in a short space of time (*sings the last line of the first verse into the chorus*). You have to take a breath big enough to get through all that so you don't end up squeezing the last ounce of breath out of your lungs to get the final words fitted in. Just being able to control that, and being aware that you're going to have to sing a long passage and taking a breath big enough at the right time, is very important.

CL: Do you find it more comfortable to work in certain keys than in others?

MU: I'm actually all right in most of them, but for some reason anything we've written in E seems to be difficult for me. It's either too low to sing with any real power, or too high to sing in the range that

I'm comfortable in. So now we're trying to avoid doing things in E. Having said that, we've actually done one in E on the new album ("U-Vox"), because the guitar used an open string tuning, which I had to play in E. Because we work on the music first, before the lyrics, we're often not quite sure how the vocal melody is going to sound until the music's done. By that time you've usually recorded most of it, so it's too late to change the key.

CL: But you obviously do think a great deal about the *structure* of the vocals.

MU: When it comes to recording, I tend to treat the voice a bit like another instrument. I'll break the vocals down into sections, just like you would layer a keyboard here or put a guitar there and the hi-hat somewhere else. And I understand the sound that the vocals should be making, like whether it's a tight, quiet, whispered sound, so the microphone's close to your mouth and you sing it incredibly quietly and you get a really nice warm whispery effect from that. So I maybe have a couple of lines sung like that and then have a soaring really high vocal come over the top of it. So you're building it up — the vocal isn't just something

Jimmy S. & The Communards

Genesis P.A. and lights in rehearsal

that you stick on at the end. It's not just the icing on the cake.

CL: Have you thought about having vocal tuition?

MU: Not really. I don't know if I'd gain anything by going to a teacher. That sounds a really crass horrible thing to say, but I really don't know if it would benefit me in any way. It might help me with my breathing, but then again it might stop me from what I do naturally. It's like when I was talking to Mick Karn (*ex-Japan*) who's a brilliant bass player. He said he doesn't know the notation of any of the notes he plays and doesn't want to learn in case he screws up his playing style. I feel sort of roughly the same way about my voice. Lessons may help me technically, but maybe I'd lose the way I do things naturally. I don't necessarily want to be over-protective towards my voice. It stands up OK and seems to do its job. That's good enough for me.

THINGS TO REMEMBER

1. Work *with* your P.A. rather than against it; use the mike as a 'volume control,' moving closer in or further away as you hit soft or loud notes.
2. Make sure you can hear yourself. If you have monitors, get the vocals mixed up loud, with perhaps the keyboards or rhythm guitar to help you keep pitch. If you don't have monitors, try angling your P.A. speakers inwards slightly, so that *you* can hear a little of what you're inflicting on your audience! Beware of feedback, though.
3. Think of the vocals as another instrument in the band. Work out the effect you want to create and plan your phrasing and mike technique accordingly.
4. Everyone has a different vocal range (see below). Your voice will sound better in some keys than in others. So work out what sounds best for you, and get the band to *transpose* a song that doesn't feel right. Remember, they are there to back you. Your voice is the main attraction!

Vocal Range

There are four standard vocal ranges: bass, tenor, alto, soprano. The male voice tends to fall into the first two, and the female voice into the latter two, although men can reach soprano through a technique known as **falsetto**, whereby you let your voice 'break' at the limit of its natural range and go into a higher — although usually weaker — register (check out anything by Frankie Valli, "Red Light" on U2's "War" album, or "Slow Love" on Prince's "Sign o' The Times" LP). But there are a very few natural male sopranos.

"I think soprano is the best description (of Jimmy Somerville's voice). If you're using a falsetto voice or counter tenor, you get that very resonant head sound — it sounds very nasal, and Jimmy doesn't really have that. It actually sounds like a chest voice, but it's very high. I really don't know — he must have something very strange happening to his larynx."
RICHARD COLES, ON FELLOW COMMUNARD JIMMY SOMERVILLE

Jimmy Somerville

Between these four ranges there are several sub-categories: **baritone** (midway between tenor and bass), **contralto** (deep alto), **mezzo-soprano** (midway between alto and soprano), and so on.

To find your range, use the diagram below in conjunction with a keyboard. *(See Fig. 75)*

BASS — middle C to C two octaves below;

TENOR — G above middle C to G two octaves below that;

ALTO — C above middle C to C below middle C;

SOPRANO — C two octaves above middle C to G below middle C.

Play middle C. Relax. Take a deep breath and sing the note, using an 'aahh' sound. Now repeat the process playing one key down from middle C. Keep stepping down a note at a time until you reach a pitch where you cannot comfortably produce a sustained sound. You've now established the bottom of your natural range. Have a short rest. Now go through the same process, this time moving **up** from middle C one note at a time until you reach a pitch where you cannot comfortably sing a sustained note any higher. You've now reached the top of your natural range. If your voice breaks into falsetto, don't go beyond that pitch for the moment. We'll come back to it.

Range and Keys

Basic range is closely allied to tonality and key preference. You may find it necessary to transpose a particular song from one key to another, to let your voice get to grips with the melody. Ultravox vocalist Midge Ure, for example, prefers not to use the key of E (see p.161). West Coast producer David Pack (Patti Austin, James Ingram), finds himself transposing songs all the time.

Don't be disappointed if to start with your range seems limited or your voice sounds weak. Practice will strengthen the muscles you need for singing and give you the confidence you need for performing. The sound of your favorite vocalist on record or on stage has also gone through a great deal of technological enhancement: reverb, double tracking, harmonizing, vocoding will all help a voice sound bigger, stronger and truer than it really is.

"Working recently with Jennifer Holliday, for example, she didn't want to scream on a piece that Mike (McDonald) and I had written for her, so we had to transpose it down. And it's amazing what a half-step down can do for a voice — it can make a whole difference to the texture and to the ear perceiving whether the singer is screaming or not — trying to hit that note when their real voice wasn't meant to go up that high."

DAVID PACK

Fig. 75

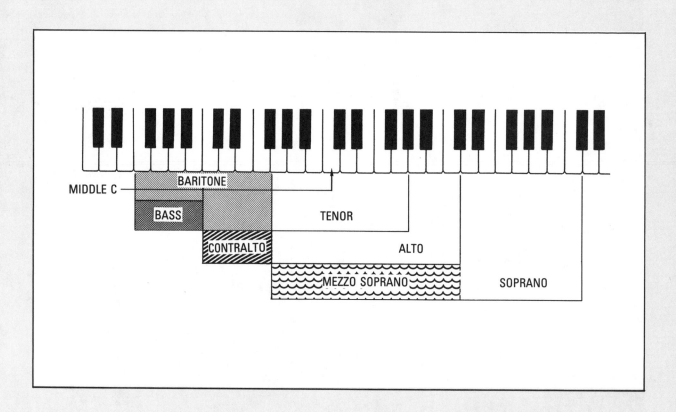

Michael McDonald, left, James Ingram, right, and friends.

IN A CLASS OF HIS OWN

Grammy award winning singer, songwriter and producer Michael McDonald first emerged in the early '70s as keyboard player for West Coast supergroup *Steely Dan*. Joining the *Doobie Brothers* in 1975, he wrote some of the band's most popular tunes, including the classic "Minute By Minute."

Since 1980, he has penned a string of massive hits, some in collaboration with other writers and singers like Kenny Loggins, James Ingram and Patti Labelle. Just check out "What a Fool Believes," "No Lookin' Back," "Ya Mo B There," "Sweet Freedom," "On My Own." The list is endless.

Something that unites all of these songs is their refreshing and effective use of vocal harmonies. Whether it be simple *oohs* and *aahs*, Gospel-like call-and-response, or more complex counterpoint, the McDonald touch is as distinctive as it is light. We spoke mainly about the basic harmony arrangement ideas common to rock and pop.

CL: What would you say are the role of harmonies in pop and rock?

MMcD: Well, for the most part, they're an orchestration and coloration of things. With the human voice you're kind of limitless with arrangement and you can cover a vast palette of sound and coloration that you can't really get with any one of the other instruments in a band. You know, a guitar's a guitar and it stays within the range of the sound of a guitar, whereas voices can cover a much wider area.

CL: What are some of the most common harmony arrangement devices that you might use in putting a song together?

MMcD: A lot of it is down to parallel three-part harmony. In rock music that seems to be the most called-on style. And you can use them in different ways. There's a *rhythmic* use that bolsters the instrumental arrangement of a song. Like in the case of ''Minute By Minute,'' it was a piano figure that I put the background vocals to. A lot of times when you have a rhythm track you might look to match the backing vocals with what one of the instruments is playing. Then there's *oohs* and *aahs*, which are more like blankets or pads. They add dimension and give you a sense of something back there, you know, instead of what's going on at the forefront.

CL: How would you orchestrate *oohs* and *aahs* on a record?

MMcD: There's a problem that you have to watch out for. *Oohs* and *aahs* can become very thick-sounding very easily and eat up all the space around them in the mix.

The Everly Brothers

One way to avoid this is to take a tip from string arrangers, who tend not to write strictly lateral parallel harmonies. So what you can do is work out the harmonies and then move one interval out of the middle either up or down until you find a voicing that's pleasing and still fits the overall voicing of the song. Now when you come to put your three voices down on tape they might sound kind of disonant. But the moment you double them up, they can sound very beautiful. With violins you have a natural resonant phasing quality when three or more are played together, which the human voice sometimes doesn't have until you double it. And all of a sudden what you'll find in your mix is you've got your pads, you've got your color back there and now you can bring the level up because your harmonies are not eating up all the space around them.

CL: Should you leave out the third if you want to avoid thick-sounding intervals?

MMcD: I don't think so — in recent years with the fusion of jazz and other influences, people have found it interesting to leave out the third. But in the earlier years of rock it was always present. It was much like Country and Gospel music — a lot of what's very exciting about Gospel is very simple three-part harmony, but with twenty voices singing it, and you know it's a very powerful thing to have twenty people singing a three-part chord. There's nothing like it, really.

CL: Another arrangement idea that is very important in your music is call and response. Could you explain how you approach that?

MMcD: Well, I guess one would be in a Gospel style where the chorus *answers* the lead vocalist, and the lead sings around the chorus, in a fixed kind of background part, a rhythmic refrain. Like "Taking It To The Streets," which was a tune we did with the Doobies.

CL: You used a similar device to a very different effect on a song you wrote with James Ingram, "Ya Mo B There."

MMcD: You're talking about the unison chanting? Yeh — both these things have a very folkish quality about them that I think comes from the African influence on

The Beach Boys

American music, in the sense that Gospel was really a kind of collision of Protestant Church music and African music. The chant on "Ya Mo" — the first line has lyrics that mean something and the second half is really just phonetics that sound and feel good. But being in unison it has a different kind of power to it that would not have come across through harmony.

CL: What would your advice be to young singers wanting to get their harmonies together?

MMcD: Obviously if you're into harmony, you should listen to a lot of records that have harmony, from early Gospel to the Beatles, the Everly Brothers, the Beach Boys, the Temptations — whoever it may be. Try to work out what it is they're singing and how they're bringing the parts in and out.

That's what we did when we were growing up — as well as singing in Church or in bands. It's also good to learn some basic things, like how to build a triad and how to make a major seventh chord. Be flexible. If three-part harmony doesn't seem like it's quite getting it, why not tuck a *fourth* voice in there — either on top or below — and that might make all the difference. Having said all that, a lot of the time what we'll actually *do* is rather than try to pre-think it we'll sing it through on tape and if someone starts doing something that sounds good, we'll all gravitate towards it. Someone might put a certain inflection in the phrasing and it becomes nice when all the harmony parts follow that inflection. But, like a lot of the best ideas, those kind of things tend to come up on the spot.

The Pointer Sisters

THINGS TO REMEMBER

1. Avoid a muddy harmony sound by planning your intervals and inversions carefully, and meshing the background voices together: move notes out of the middle area occupied by the lead vocal, and think about synchronizing vibrato, phrasing and expression.
2. Don't be afraid to use a major third, but remember other intervals that can give a dramatic effect, like the sixth or flattened seventh.
3. Try out different harmony arrangements: *oohs* and *aahs* for quietly building passages; three — or four — part parallel for emphasizing choruses or hook lines; call-and-response for a soulful feel or a dance groove; and more complex 'pyramid' or counterpoint arrangements.
4. But there are no hard and fast rules. Do what your ears tell you to!

PYRAMID HARMONIES

Pyramid harmonies have been around in rock for a long time, although in their classic form they are most associated with rock'n'roll of the '50s and '60s. For example, you can hear them used on Danny and The Juniors' 1957 hit "At The Hop," on The Beatles' "Twist and Shout," and on The Beach Boys' "Barbaran."

The idea is for a number of voices to come in at staggered intervals, each building up towards a unison peak in the song. In the examples mentioned above, the lead voice comes in singing the root note, a second voice comes in on the major third, and another voice comes in on the fifth, together creating a basic triad chord: *(See Fig. 76)*

You can go on adding notes like the seventh, octave root, or even the ninth. (Check out, for example, Grandmaster Flash and Melle Mel's anti-coke classic, "White Lines".) *(Fig. 77)*

Another idea is to **reverse** the pyramid, your voices starting in unison and descending in steps to separate harmonies. This creates the effect of the vocals 'blossoming out,' and can be heard in the middle section of "Bohemian Rhapsody" by Queen (on the line "Let him go!"). Here's a simple example of a reverse pyramid idea. Try practicing this with the other singers in your band: *(See Fig. 78)*

Danny and The Juniors

Fig. 76

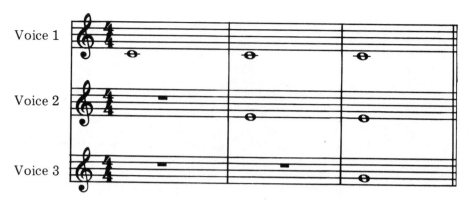

Fig. 77

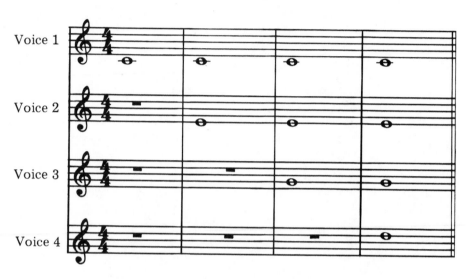

Fig. 78

COUNTERPOINT

This is a more sophisticated device that has its origins in opera and orchestral music (check out the Brandenburg Concertos by J.S. Bach or the "Song of Songs" by Palestrina). Counterpoint usually consists of two or more separate melodic lines, which, when played or sung simultaneously, create a harmonic whole. You can hear classic *vocal* examples of this including songs by the Beatles ("Eleanor Rigby," "She's Leaving Home"), and the Mamas and Papas ("California Dreaming," "Monday Monday").

Below is a simple example for two voices.

Notice how the two melodies interweave and seem to 'chase' each other. *(See Fig. 79)*

The Commodores

Fig. 79

5

The Police

Song Structure and Arrangements

Introduction

By way of an epilogue, let's briefly consider one or two basic aspects of song structure and arrangement. No matter how advanced your playing and programming techniques, or how great your vocal skills, it won't count for much if at the end of the day you've got a muddy sound and a rambling song that's going nowhere.

Song structure deals with how you put a song *together* — how many verses and choruses, do you have an instrumental break, and so on. Arrangement deals more with how you put a song *across*. This involves deciding on the feel or style of the backing — for example, is it funky or straight-ahead rock; is it music to dance to or for sitting cross-legged to in the middle of the room?

Structure

Song structures can vary enormously. But there are certain basic elements that often appear. Pop songs, for example, tend to be fairly short, say about three minutes long, and consist of at least two different sections — a verse and a chorus — repeated several times over. A verse might last for 16 bars and be played over a repeated two-chord pattern. A change of chord would lead the ear into the chorus. This would probably be shorter, more repetitive, and hopefully the bit that people go around humming because it's so catchy.

But there's often more to a pop tune than that. Another commonly favored section is called the 'Middle Eight.' Not surprisingly, this often lasts for eight bars and comes in the middle of the song. It acts as a release from the constant repetition of verse/chorus, using different chords — perhaps derived from the key scale chord family (see p.183) — and would either feature a different set of lyrics or be used as an instrumental section, or a mixture of both. A typical example is shown below. The chorus is of a standard C, F, and G configuration. Via the chord of E minor, things move smoothly into a middle eight of A minor, F, and G, leading back to the chorus again after eight bars: *(See Fig. 80)*

Fig. 80

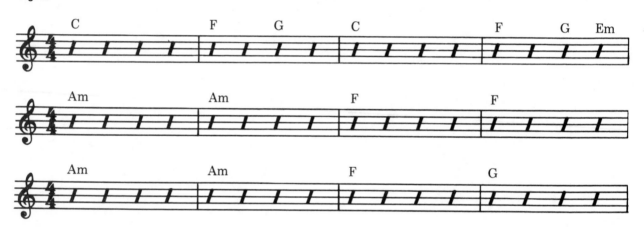

Dance records, meanwhile, may replace the middle eight with a 'breakdown' (see p.180), which might feature percussion, electronic effects, chants and so on. Breakdowns can go on for almost any period of time — especially on 12-inch extended mixes!

Other basic structural features include the 'intro' and 'outro,' the 'bridge' and the 'riff.' Rock numbers might use a repeated chord figure to double as an intro and then as a bridge between verse/chorus sections (listen out for this on Van Halen's "Jump," or the Rolling Stones' "Brown Sugar"). An outro might simply consist of the chorus or bridge repeated until the fade (on a record) or until a punctuated ending (in live performance). The riff, meanwhile, is a time-honored device in rock that can be used as an intro, bridge, or indeed as the basis for an entire song (for more on riffs and how to create them, see the companion volume to this book, *ROCK-SCHOOL — Guitar, Bass, Drums*).

Arrangement

There is an infinite number of ways to play the same piece of music. In the end only you and the rest of the band can decide what sounds right for your song. Having said that, arrangement can be broken down into two broad areas — orchestration and rhythmic deployment.

In rock there are, broadly speaking, two main aspects to orchestration: working out combinations of different sounds and deciding which go well together, and structuring your chords and melodies to suit these sounds. In other words, orchestration is about working out instrumental *voices* and chord *voicings*. A chord voicing depends on the vertical placement of the notes and whether you double up any of them or leave any out. The sound and style with which you're working may help you determine how

Orchestration

"The important thing is to find your own frequencies. If you've got a guitar in the band, you know that there are certain frequencies you should steer clear of. If you're playing big chords behind the vocals, you would usually keep them more mellow so that the voice can still cut through. The tendency nowadays is to keep sounds small and spiky and isolated, but rich layered chords still have their place. It's just a question of working out when to use them."

TONY BANKS

you voice a chord. On a guitar, for example, if you play a full D7 chord, the voicing looks like this: (See Fig. 81)

Fig. 81

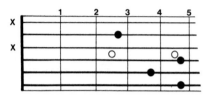

Played with a clean sound, the harmony rings through. Played with a heavy sustain sound, the same chord will sound messy, because distortion 'thickens up' individual notes by emphasizing harmonics and overtones that will clash when too many are played at once. If you strip down the chord, leaving out the third and flattened seventh and playing only the first, fifth and octave, it'll sound much cleaner and spacier. What you end up with is a D5 or D *power chord*: (See Fig. 82)

Fig. 82

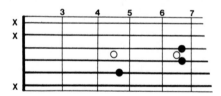

With synths and keyboards, this question of matching voicings with instrumental voices becomes even more involved, because of the huge number of different sounds at your disposal.

As well as using partial chords to create a cleaner sound, you can make a very simple chord sound more interesting by choosing unusual bass notes underneath. Played against an A minor chord, for example, a D bass note would create a D9, an F would make an F major7, an A would create a straight A minor, and a C would make a C6. Within the framework of one basic chord, you've created a very moody sequence. The Police are one group who have made this device their hallmark. You can hear it most effectively used on tracks like "Da Do Do Do," "Can't

Stand Losing You," and "Don't Stand So Close To Me."

This brings us to one of the most effective and most frequently used harmonic ideas in rock — the pedal note (named after the piano sustain pedal). By keeping one instrument constant while others change over the top, you can create a feeling of enormous tension. The bass, for example, could keep pumping away on one note — say a D — while the guitar and keyboards play D major root position, followed by first inversion F major, and then first inversion G major. The Who used this idea to great effect on tracks like "Bell Boy" from the 1973 LP "Quadrophenia." But other stadium bands, such as U2 and Genesis, are also fond of pedal notes and chords.

Here are a couple of simple pedal note ideas. Firstly, against a bass playing low A eighth notes, play two bars of A major, followed by two bars of B7, followed by two bars of B♭ major seventh, one bar of C major (against a C root), and one bar split between G major and D major, bringing you back to the A again.

Secondly, a low F played in a dotted rhythm. Try the following chords: F major second inversion; root position C minor; Dm7 leading with the seventh; C# major seventh, also leading with the seventh; and then back to the F once more. Keyboard players may find these chord configurations easier to handle than guitarists!

Of course, modifying chords can be a complex process, involving a thorough knowledge of musical theory (see, for example, the section on Modes, p.183). But don't be put off. Try putting *any* chord sequence you know against a constant bass note — perhaps a note that appears in all the chords — and see what you come up with. Experimentation is a key part of extending your knowledge of chords and scales.

Rhythmic Deployment

Rhythmic deployment is another major aspect of arrangement and

"I found that playing keyboards in rock, especially if you're going for that urgent distorted lead sound, and you try to play chords — you have to get away from triads. I usually play just two notes, but by using distortion and then maybe a bass note played by another instrument, I can create the illusion of a more complex chord. But it all happens within the distortion."
JAN HAMMER

style, and this is sometimes underestimated in comparison to the harmonic and melodic content of a song. The instruments in a band all have rhythmic parts to play, which, when locked together, help to create an overall feel or recognizable style. For this to happen, each musician must try not to mask the rhythm patterns of the other instruments, but to enhance them. This might involve a degree of duplication, maybe a little syncopation around the main rhythm, or simply shutting up to let the others be heard.

Take the classic example of a reggae one-drop. The feel is 'up-in-the-air,' largely because the bass drum doesn't play on the first beat of the bar, but 'drops' on the three. The rhythm guitar and piano play a clipped 'shank' on the two and four — the *up* beats. So what's left to hold the rhythm down? The bass guitar, which may play a two-bar riff starting on beat one of bar one and ending on beat three of bar two. Every instrument fulfills its own rhythmic role and dovetails with the others to produce a feel that is unmistakable:
(See Fig. 83)

"A guy in America once said that the most distinctive thing about my playing was that I always seem to use the wrong bass note for the chord. If I played a B♭ chord, for instance, instead of playing a B♭ bass, I would play an E♭. It makes the chord different to what you think it is, because a chord is defined by its bass note."
TONY BANKS

In rock, what you *don't* play can be as important as what you *do*!

Fig. 83

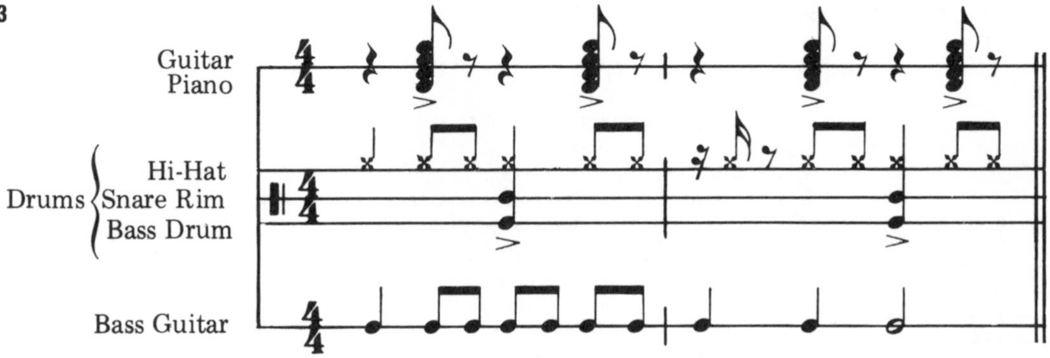

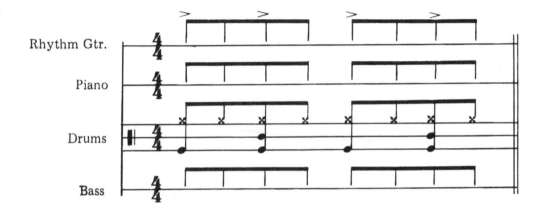

The opposite extreme might be found in a straight-ahead rock'n'roll tune, where the predominant feel is of all the instruments truckin' along together in unison. For this the rhythmic scheme might be:

Fig. 84

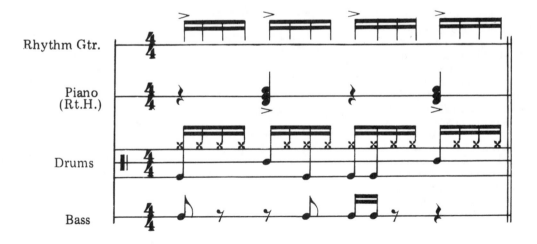

Completely different from reggae!

Rhythmic unison can be very effective and exciting. But it can also become predictable and sluggish if over-used. Many rock players, therefore, take their cue from the rhythmic deployment within the drum kit to suggest rhythmic band parts. So, the bass guitar might follow the bass drum (or vice versa); a scratchy rhythm guitar might echo the feel of the hi-hat part; and solid right hand block chords from the piano might bolster the snare. The result would be something like this:

Fig. 85

Selwyn Brown

"When reggae started originally, it was constructed mostly on the piano and organ. So keyboards were very important — playing a basic shuffle or bubble — with the horns on top and the drums and bass grooving together underneath, and the guitar just skanking along. Then in the '70s we started using other little things like the MiniMoog, and to take our inspiration from other styles of music. And nowadays we'll go into the studio, lay down the basic tracks with either a drum machine or a real drummer and a bass line, and then start building on top of that with synths. Sometimes it might be a Rhodes-type thing, or maybe a warm flute sound. Then we might go on to more synthetic sounds, using samplers. It's just to decorate the music, you know. But however much we bring in other influences, we keep the roots, because the bass and the drums and the skank are still there."
                                              SELWYN BROWN

Effective though this groove might be, it can also become mechanical. So we get back to the reggae example again, where each instrument has its own rhythmic space and all the patterns lock together to produce the complete rhythm. Each instrument supports and enhances the others.

All good bands, no matter what their style, develop this sort of instrumental empathy. So, for instance, the bass drum and bass guitar underpin, coax, and support one another, aware of each other's rhythm, but not necessarily coinciding with every note. The rhythm guitar doesn't have to duplicate the hi-hat exactly; it could play broken up sixteenths, leaving the hi-hat to be less busy, but more syncopated. The keyboards could play sustained pads, occasionally accenting or stabbing in unison with the drums and/or bass. The following is a rhythmic breakdown of a fairly complicated funk groove. Note how each instrument has its own rhythm and space, but locks in and complements the others. *(See Fig. 86)*

If you get stuck for ideas on new rhythms and feels, try listening to Latin and Caribbean styles. After all, much of the syncopation in modern music can be traced to forms such as Cuban Cha-cha-cha, Rumba and Mambo; Brazilian Bossa Nova or Samba; Trinidadian Calypso, and so on.

Fig. 86

Rhythmic Development and Variation

Everyone occasionally gets stuck in a rut playing the same old rhythms. Sometimes, when presented with a new song, it's difficult to come up with a new or suitable rhythm. A good rule of thumb — as with drum machines also — is to start with the simplest rhythm that works. You can then experiment by adding extra touches here and there until everything's in the right place. Don't go mad and desperately throw in every rhythm you

know at the beginning. You'll only make things worse.

So, how do you develop a rhythm? Well, the rhythmic deployment idea works here too. A song or riff might suggest phrases to you which can be tried on different parts of the kit and elaborated in countless ways. More often than not, the snare drum will fall on the two and four, but can occasionally be syncopated and given a more flowing feel by the addition of softer 'inside' beats. The bass drum can also play many different

rhythms, while the hi-hat, being the lightest, is perhaps the most flexible part of the kit and can be used to suggest very different feels.

The following examples are all based on one simple two-bar pattern — defined by the snare drum and bass drum, which remain almost constant throughout. Most of the variation comes from the changes in the hi-hat, and the eventual introduction of the ride cymbal. *(See Fig. 87)*

Fig. 87

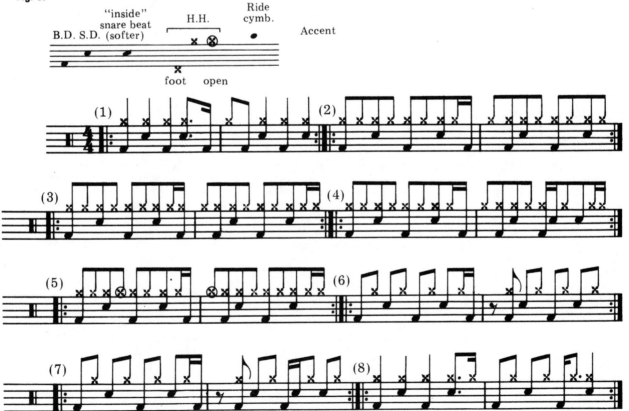

As you can see, the number of variations on a single rhythm are pretty well inexhaustible. And although some of those above may seem a bit elaborate, they can always be used to back up a solo or to pile it on towards the end of the song. Or you could use some as fills to get from one section of the song to the next without losing the groove.

Intros, Breakdowns and Dynamics
During introductions or 'break-down' sections, other rhythmic ideas may occur to you. The possibilities are enormous and entirely dependent upon your own ingenuity and taste, but for illustration, below are a few ideas — again based on the two-bar pattern used earlier.

A common intro device is that of a stripped-down or spaced-out verion of the main rhythm, so that tension is built up ready for the dynamic entry of the song proper.

To do this, try using just the bass drum, or the hi-hat, or the snare. Maybe some delicate percussion or cymbal sounds would be more appropriate, leaving room to come in with a dramatic fill, or indeed straight into the rhythm without warning.

The examples here are of the 'stripped-down' variety, culminating in a fill still suggestive of the two-bar rhythm:
(See Fig. 88)

Fig. 88

(5) Last two bars of intro.

A breakdown may involve a similar sort of approach. Or, by contrast, you might try *intensifying* the rhythm, using extra rhythmic parts and percussion to take over from the dropped-out vocal and instrumental parts. On dance records, elaborate percussive breaks often feature outrageous sampled sounds, reverb and echo effects, 'impossible' bass drum figures and so on, usually supplied by drum machines, sequencers and other digital gadgetry.

The following examples may suggest some ideas for live performance or recording.

The first set of rhythms below are based on 'ago-go' bell and cowbell rhythms to overdub on the basic groove. They can be adapted to suit all sorts of different sounds and instruments. With a little thought, they can even be played on the kit while keeping the basic beat going. This is just one example of how the percussion rhythms of Latin music are used to spice up rock and funk.
(See Fig. 89)

Fig. 89   **Breakdown Sections-Percussive Breaks**

The next set of examples involve sixteenth note bass drum fills around the basic pattern. There are many ways of re-creating this sort of effect live: by using a double bass drum pedal, or even double bass drums; by playing a floor tom and single bass drum; or by 'cheating' with an electronic bass drum patch routed to a pad played with one or both hands. In this last case, you could then try playing snare and hi-hat with just the left hand; that would leave the right foot free to play even more bass drum, or if your bass drum is an electronic pad, to play whatever sound you had routed to it.

Nowadays, almost anything's possible. Have fun!

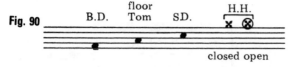

MELODIC SOLOING IDEAS

Finally, let's look at an area of playing that presents one of the most exciting challenges a musician can face: soloing. A solo is, of course, made up of a series of notes; and the notes you choose to play can be derived from a number of different musical sources.

You're probably playing against some kind of harmonic backing — a chord sequence or a riff. This will be played in a particular key. And so right away you can choose notes for your solo from the key scale of the backing. One way of creating a feeling of energy and excitement is to play the chord sequence as a series of *arpeggios*, with different accents and rhythms.

This might not give you the feeling you want. But fear not. There are alternatives. You may remember that in the first *ROCKSCHOOL* book we talked about one of the most widely used solo voices in rock — the blues scale. This is a very important part of the rock sound, but flexible though it is, there is a danger of sounding repetitive and dull if you overuse it. So how do you keep your solos fresh and inventive? Well, let's go back to scales for a moment. If you take the major scale in the key of your song, but play it starting on a note other than the root note, you might start to hear new melodic patterns.

Modes

This idea holds the key to fresh and inventive soloing based on patterns of notes called **Modes**. A mode is a displaced scale. There are seven modes, and the tonality of each comes from the C major scale — the white notes on the piano. Each mode starts on a different note of the C major scale.

The sound of each mode is different, because each has a unique pattern of tones and semi-tones. And, of course, once you've worked out this pattern, you can play it in any key. The names of the modes derive from ancient Greek scales (see diagram below). *(See Fig. 91)*

Fig. 91

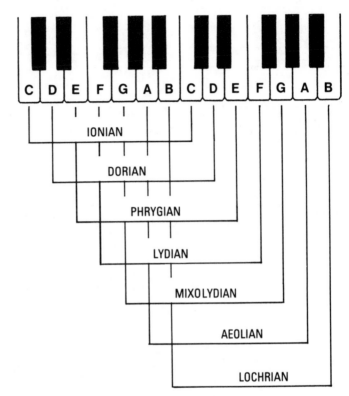

Fig. 92

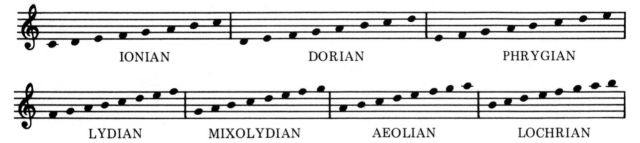

Modes of the C Major Scale

IONIAN   DORIAN   PHRYGIAN

LYDIAN   MIXOLYDIAN   AEOLIAN   LOCHRIAN

But you don't have to stay in the key of C to use modes. The sound characteristics of each mode can be played in any key, as long as its original step pattern is not changed.

PLAYED FROM		NAME	PATTERN OF TONES & SEMITONES							
C — C'	1-8	IONIAN	1W	2W	3H	4W	5W	6W	7H	8
D — D'	2-9	DORIAN	2W	3H	4W	5W	6W	7H	8W	9
E — E'	3-10	PHRYGIAN	3H	4W	5W	6W	7H	8W	9W	10
F — F'	4-11	LYDIAN	4W	5W	6W	7H	8W	9W	10H	11
G — G'	5-12	MIXOLYDIAN	5W	6W	7H	8W	9W	10H	11W	12
A — A'	6-13	AEOLIAN	6W	7H	8W	9W	10H	11W	12W	13
B — B'	7-14	LOCRIAN	7H	8W	9W	10H	11W	12W	13W	14

Let's see where these notes would fit on the guitar and bass, using the C scale as our example:

Fig. 93

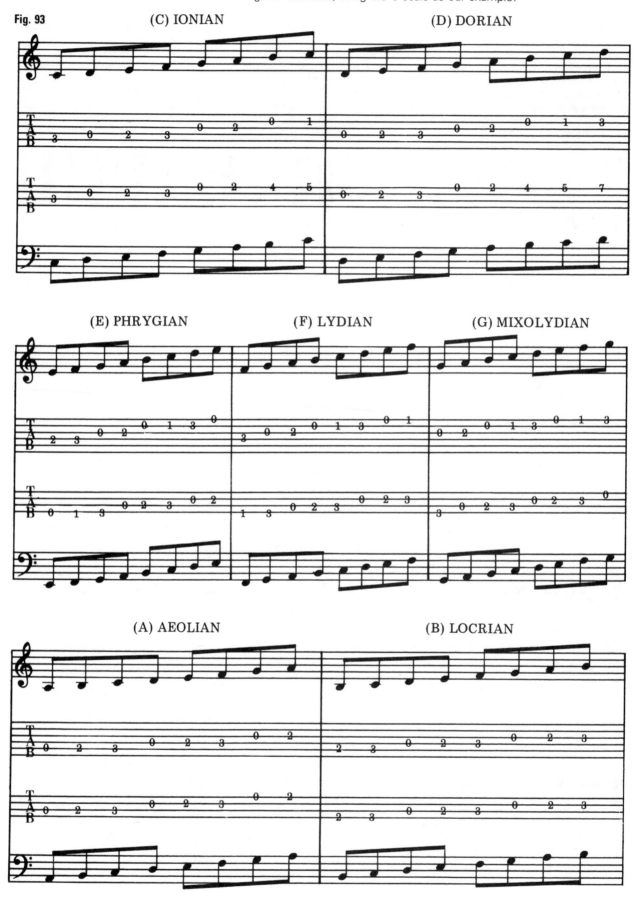

Practice playing the modes in sequence and once you feel comfortable, translate them into all the other keys.

Modal Solos

To use these modes in your soloing, you have to relate them to *chords*. Try playing the first, third, fifth and seventh notes of your mode. You'll notice that they make up familiar sounding chords.

STEP	SCALE/ TONE	INTERVALS	CHORD
1	1, 3, 5, 7	R, MA 3rd, PER 5th, MA 7th	C△
2	2, 4, 8, 10	R, MI 3rd, PER 5th, MI 7th	Dm⁷
3	3, 5, 7, 9	R, MI 3rd, PER 5th, MI 7th	Em⁷
4	4, 6, 8, 10	R, MA 3rd, PER 5th, MA 7th	F△
5	5, 7, 9, 11	R, MA 3rd, PER 5th, MI 7th	G⁷
6	6, 8, 10, 12	R, MI 3rd, PER 5th, MI 7th	Am⁷
7	7, 9, 11, 13	R, MI 3rd, 5th, MI 7th	Bm⁷ᴰ⁵

*R = root   MA = major   Per = Perfect
MI = minor   △ = major 7th.

In fact, if we analyze the chords created, we have a pattern of seventh chords built on the tones that fall naturally within the major scale, i.e., the major chord family (for more information on major scale chords, refer to our companion volume *ROCKSCHOOL — Guitar, Bass, Drums*).

Fig. 94   IONIAN   DORIAN   PHRYGIAN   LYDIAN   MIXO—LYDIAN   AEOLIAN   LOCRIAN
solo line   etc.

Cmaj7   Dm7   Em7   Fmaj7   G7   Am7   Bm7♭5

Each mode can be used as a solo line against its respective chord in the family group. Try recording a backing tape of — or getting a friend to play — the major chord family in sequence. Then make up short phrases on each mode against its respective chord. Once you've mastered this in C, transpose the chords and phrases into other keys. Let's take the Dorian mode as an example, starting on the D note. To find out which chord this might go well with, play the first, third, fifth and seventh notes of the mode and what you get is the notes of a D minor seventh chord — D, F, A and C.

Let's look at how this relates to playing the guitar and improvising over certain chord sequences, by examining the three most commonly used modes in rock and jazz: the Aeolian, Dorian and Mixolydian.

Aeolian

This is the name given to the mode starting on the sixth degree of the major scale. It contains the same notes as the natural or *relative minor* scale. *(See Fig. 95)*

Fig. 95

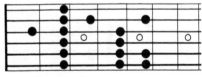

Moveable shapes
—Root note on 6th string

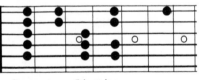

—Root note on 5th string

Basic principles: All major chords take the Ionian mode as a solo line unless they contain a flattened fifth or an 11th, then the Lydian mode is used;

All dominant chords take the Mixolydian mode as a solo line;

All minor chords take the Dorian mode as a solo line unless the chord sequence has a strong minor feel, in which case the Aeolian mode is used.

Once you've mastered the basics, you'll probably ignore all this!

Fig. 96

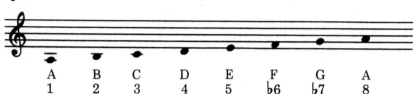

A	B	C	D	E	F	G	A
1	2	3	4	5	♭6	♭7	8

Record or sequence the following chords, or get a friend to play them for you. Play ideas based on the appropriate Aeolian mode over each chord sequence.

You'll find that the pentatonic blues scale will work over any of these chord sequences. Modes can give you more subtle and interesting sounds, but you'll have to be more discriminating in their use, for example changing mode as the chords change. This involves working out the key or *tonal center* of your backing and establishing the relationship of the chords to it. Below are two straightforward I, IV, V sequences, respectively in the key of C major and G major, with an A minor chord tacked onto the end of each. But in the first, A minor figures as a VI chord — and here the Aeolian mode would be appropriate; in the second, it figures as a II chord — with a more 'minor' feel appropriate to the use of the Dorian mode.
(See Fig. 100)

Fig. 97

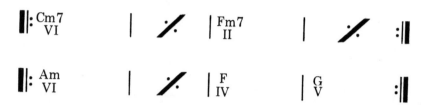

Dorian

This is the mode starting on the second degree of the major scale.

It is minor in feel, as it contains a flattened third.

Mixolydian Mode

This is the mode starting on the fifth degree of the major scale. You might find it easier to think of it as a 'major scale,' but with a flattened (dominant) seventh note. Not unsurprisingly, it sounds good against dominant seventh chords.
(See Fig. 101)

Fig. 98

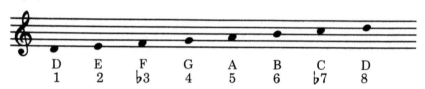

D	E	F	G	A	B	C	D
1	2	♭3	4	5	6	♭7	8

Root note starting on 6th string

Root note on 6th string

Root note starting on 5th string

Try the Dorian mode over the following chord sequences:

Root note on 5th string

Fig. 99

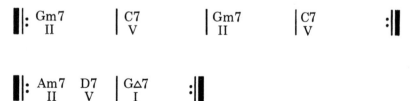

Fig. 102

Over this sequence use
A mixolydian mode

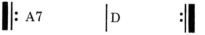

Fig. 100

‖: C
    I | F
                 IV   :‖: G
                              V | Am
                                       VI   :‖

‖: G
    I | C
                 IV   :‖: D
                              V | Am
                                       II   :‖

"When it comes to scales and chords, I find it's important to practice them in every key. Because, especially with the way the keyboard's set out, certain scales are easier to play than others. And another thing is to incorporate practicing into your songwriting. If I learn a new chord, for example, I'll try to put it into a new song so that I'm always working on it."
SELWYN BROWN

More Advanced Soloing Ideas

Practicing scales is a really good if slightly boring way of building up your technique, familiarizing yourself with the keyboard or fingerboard, and developing your ear. With reference to the last point, it's especially good to practice scales in the context of hearing them over different chord sequences, as already suggested above.

However, to get the most out of scale practice, you should try to make them sound more 'musical' — break them down into smaller sections that could be used in a solo or melody.

All the following examples use the C major scale, but you should try them with different scales and also the modes we've looked at (see p. 183). The first example

breaks down the scale into groups of three notes; the second into groups of four. Example three is more difficult, as it uses the scale as a series of arpeggios or broken chords. Take it slowly at first and concentrate on getting a smooth, fluent sound. Example four is similar, but adds a third to the pattern so that you play the seventh scale tone chords as arpeggios. *(Fig. 103)*

Fig. 103

TWO WAYS OF NAMING MODES

D Dorian mode — means start on D playing the major scale of which D is the second degree, i.e., the C major scale;

Dorian mode *key of D* — means play the scale of D major starting on its second degree, i.e., starting on the note of E.

Confused? Just wait 'til the band starts playing!

OK, we've given you some ideas on expression, dynamics, phrasing and notes. But how do you put all this together in a coherent shape? How do you *construct* a solo? At its simplest, I suppose, a solo builds up to an apex and then builds down again. But it all depends on the context of the solo,

"First and foremost I see myself as a songwriter, and the main thing I'm interested in is writing accompaniments. So when I play lead, I look upon my solos as more like little instrumentals — played melodies. And I write them as carefully as I would a vocal tune."

TONY BANKS

and the feeling you want to get. You could instead start on a long impassioned high note, or with a really flashy lick to get the audience's attention, and take it down from there.

Another common way of developing a solo is by repeating a number of different licks in different ways, as *motifs*. This can be very powerful, especially if you vary the repetition slightly — play the motif higher or lower, using different intervals and different rhythms.

Working in this way, a lot of players build up a mental catalogue of licks — guitarists have the blues scale box positions, for example — and although there's a danger of over reliance on the same old phrases, if you try playing your

licks backwards, or changing the order of the notes in some other way, you can still come up with something sounding fresh. Not everyone likes to work in this improvisational way, however.

Soloing doesn't have to be difficult. Ideas for expression and phrasing can come from the vocals in your band, and ideas for dynamics cued from the other instruments. Sound can be enhanced by use of effects. You can plan out what you're going to play, or just improvise. And if you get stuck for inspiration, you can always dip into a little musical theory to see if there are any suitable weird scales lurking about. But remember, there are no rules about what makes a great solo. That's up to you.

Well that's about it for this second ROCKSCHOOL book. We hope we've given you a few ideas on getting some interesting sounds together for your band, and answered a few basic questions for keyboard players, guitarists, bassists, drummers and vocalists. But of course, we're only here to tell you how we do it or how a few name players do it. And the great thing about rock music is that it's only important how you do it. So don't get too hung up on theory. Use it to get you around problems, but don't get swamped by it. Remember, if it *feels* right, it's going to *sound* right.

School's out.

GOODBYE

We have made every effort to trace the ownership of all copyrighted material and to secure permission from copyright holders. In the event of any question arising out of the use of any material, we will be pleased to make the necessary corrections in future printings.

PICTURE CREDITS

THE FOLLOWING ROCKSCHOOL PRODUCTS ARE AVAILABLE IN RETAIL STORES
AND DIRECTLY FROM ROCKSCHOOL:

**To Order By Phone
Call 1-800-451-7020 (Have your Mastercard or Visa ready)

To order by mail send check or money order to:

Rockschool/WNET
P.O. Box 68618
Indianapolis, Indiana 46268

Add $2 per item shipping and handling

<u>VIDEOCASSETTES</u> (Hosted by Herbie Hancock—approximately 1 hour each)
Volume 1: Elementary Equipment and Basic Technique
   For guitar, bass, and drums—choosing, tuning, and playing your instrument; effects pedals, amplification, and more. **$19.95**

Volume 2: Blues to Heavy Metal
   Explores the simplicity and subtlety of the blues, the speed and flash of heavy metal. **$19.95**

Volume 3: Funk, Reggae, and New Music
   Vital techniques and characteristics of these influential genres. **$19.95**

Volume 4: Digital-Age Hardware
   Introduction to synthesizers, sequencers, sampling, M.I.D.I., and other electronic-music innovations. **$19.95**

Volume 5: Melody and Soloing
   Tips for keyboards, vocals, guitar, drums, and bass on how to achieve strong lead lines and expressive solo breaks. **$19.95**

Volume 6: Arrangements—Putting It All Together
   Getting the most from your group—song structure, vocal and instrumental harmonies, advanced rhythm backings, etc. **$19.95**

<u>BOOKS</u>
Rockschool I: Guitar, Bass and Drums
   Instrumental technique and theory for the traditional rock "power trio." Explores the range of rock styles—blues, heavy metal, funk, reggae, and new music—with tips from internationally-acclaimed rock artists. 192 pages . . . **$9.95**

Rockschool II: Electronics, Keyboards and Vocals
   One-handed and two-handed keyboard technique, solo and group vocal technique, and a complete review of synthesizers, sequencers, sampling, M.I.D.I., and other electronic innovations behind today's music. 192 pages . . . **$9.95**